ECONOMIC ISSUES, PROBLEMS AND PERSPECTIVES

# TAX GAPS

# REDUCTION STRATEGIES, COMPLIANCE EFFORTS AND LEGISLATIVE PROPOSALS

# Economic Issues, Problems and Perspectives

Additional books in this series can be found on Nova's website under the Series tab.

Additional E-books in this series can be found on Nova's website under the E-book tab.

# American Political, Economic, and Security Issues

Additional books in this series can be found on Nova's website under the Series tab.

Additional E-books in this series can be found on Nova's website under the E-book tab.

ECONOMIC ISSUES, PROBLEMS AND PERSPECTIVES

# TAX GAPS

# REDUCTION STRATEGIES, COMPLIANCE EFFORTS AND LEGISLATIVE PROPOSALS

RONDELL MEINKE
EDITOR

nova publishers
*New York*

For permission to use material from this book please contact us:
Telephone 631-231-7269; Fax 631-231-8175
Web Site: http://www.novapublishers.com



**Library of Congress Cataloging-in-Publication Data**

ISBN: 978-1-62417-452-0

*Published by Nova Science Publishers, Inc. † New York*

# CONTENTS

# PREFACE

Recent and projected large federal budget deficits have generated congressional and executive branch interest in increasing revenue by reducing the tax gap. Specific methods for lowering the tax gap may also be used as revenue offsets under the Pay-As-You-Go Act (PAYGO). Other motivations for reducing tax gaps include adverse effects on (1)public trust in the fairness of the tax system, which may adversely affect voluntary compliance with tax laws, and (2) economic efficiency, by providing an incentive for inputs of labor and capital to shift to those sectors of the economy with greater opportunities to evade taxes. This book defines tax gap concepts, explains the methodology used to estimate the tax gap, discusses the relationship between the tax gap and enforcement, explains the Internal Revenue Service's (IRS's) strategic priorities, examines the IRS return prepayer initiative, and describes proposed legislation in the 112th Congress.

Chapter 1 – Recent and projected large federal budget deficits and the need for revenue offsets under the Pay-As-You-Go Act (PAYGO) have generated congressional interest in the feasibility of increasing revenue by reducing the tax gap. The Internal Revenue Service (IRS) defines the *gross* tax gap as the difference between the tax liability imposed by law for a given tax year and the amount of tax that taxpayers pay *voluntarily* and on time for that year. It defines the *net* tax gap as the amount of the gross tax gap that remains unpaid after all enforced and other late payments are made for the tax year. For tax (calendar) year 2006 (the most recent year for which data are available), the IRS estimated a gross tax gap of $450 billion, equal to a noncompliance rate of 16.9%. For the same tax year, IRS enforcement activities, coupled with other late payments, recovered about $65 billion of the gross tax gap, resulting in an estimated net tax gap of $385 billion. The estimated gross tax gap of $450 billion consisted of underreporting of tax liability ($376 billion), nonfiling of tax returns ($28 billion), and underpayment of taxes ($46 billion). (Taxes on illegal activities are excluded from these estimates.) Most of the underreporting of tax liability concerned underreporting of individual income liability ($235 billion). The percentage of individual income that was underreported varied significantly depending on the degree of information reporting and whether or not withholding was required. For the 2006 tax gap estimate, the IRS primarily utilized data from the National Research Program (NRP), which seeks to obtain the optimal balance among research quality, efficiency, and the reduction of taxpayer burden. Estimates of the gross tax gap have been heavily publicized; perhaps as a result, some public officials have emphasized better enforcement of tax laws in order to raise revenue. Three factors affect the dollar amount that can be collected by increased enforcement: some types of unreported income are difficult to detect, some of the detected tax liability cannot be easily collected, and many detected tax liabilities are small relative to enforcement costs. From FY2001 to FY2011, enforcement revenues collected by the IRS increased from $33.8 billion to $55.2 billion. Also from FY2001 to FY2011, IRS staffing for key enforcement occupations rose from 20,203 to 22,184. Over the past four years, the IRS has focused on six strategy priorities: technology modernization, tax return preparers, data analytics, taxpayer service, offshore tax evasion, and workforce job satisfaction. The pursuit of most of these priorities reduces the tax gap. The IRS has put in place the major facets of its tax return preparer initiative. In the 112$^{th}$ Congress, legislation concerning tax compliance has been introduced in the following seven areas: repeal of the 1099 reporting requirement (H.R. 4); identity theft (S. 1534, S. 3432, H.R. 3215, H.R. 3482, and H.R. 6205); free file (S. 1796 and H.R. 2569); contracting (H.R. 829); insurance companies (S. 1693 and H.R. 3157); tax havens (S. 1346, H.R. 2669, S. 2075, and H.R. 3338); and tax avoidance by expatriates (S. 3205).

Chapter 2 – Chairman Platts, Ranking Member Towns and Members of the Subcommittee on Government Organization, Efficiency and Financial Management, my name is Steven Miller and I am the Deputy Commissioner for Services and Enforcement at the Internal Revenue Service. I appreciate the opportunity to testify on the important issue of the tax gap, and discuss actions that the IRS is taking to improve voluntary compliance with our nation's tax laws. The tax gap is the difference between the amount of tax imposed on taxpayers for a given year and the amount that is paid voluntarily and timely. The tax gap represents, in dollar terms, the annual amount of noncompliance with our tax laws. While no system can ever achieve 100 percent compliance, the IRS has been and remains committed to finding ways to increase compliance. The IRS recently released an updated tax gap study covering the tax year 2006 which shows that the nation's compliance rate for that year of 83.1 percent is essentially unchanged from the last review covering tax year 2001. The report also showed that the net tax gap in dollars for 2006 was $385 billion. In terms of what makes up the tax gap, the underreporting of business income by individual taxpayers – income of sole proprietors, farmers and those earning rental, royalty, partnership and S Corporation income – is the largest contributor, accounting for $122 billion of the total in 2006. That is because this income, for which little or no reporting is required for income tax purposes, is the least adequately reported. We at the IRS are often asked what actions we are taking to close the tax gap. I include in my testimony a number of initiatives, from providing taxpayer services to individuals and businesses grappling with a complex tax code, to running targeted compliance and enforcement programs to address a wide variety of compliance issues. But it is important to understand that while the tax gap is a helpful guide to the scale of tax compliance in the economy, it greatly overstates the amount of deficit reduction that could be achieved through IRS enforcement alone. In other words, it is unrealistic to imagine that IRS enforcement revenues, which stood at $55.2 billion for FY 2011, could grow to a level that would close the net tax gap ($385 billion). Further, major attempts to close the gap must be considered within a context that considers taxpayer burden and taxpayer rights. At the same time, targeted investments in IRS enforcement such as those included in the Administration's FY 2013 budget request have a high return on investment and serve to improve overall compliance. Steady increases in enforcement resources applied to well-founded examination and collection programs, coupled with increases in selected third-party reporting requirements, are proven cost-effective means of reducing the tax gap. We also should not lose sight of the fact that failures to comply with tax law often involve unintentional mistakes that are the result of not fully understanding what has come to be an extremely complex tax code. For that reason, a truly comprehensive strategy to increase tax compliance must also include programs to educate taxpayers in their tax obligations and efforts at improving customer service, to make it easier for individuals and businesses to fulfill filing requirements. In its efforts to address the tax gap and improve tax compliance, the IRS follows four guiding principles: Both unintentional taxpayer errors and intentional taxpayer evasion should be addressed; Sources of noncompliance should be targeted with specificity; Enforcement activities should be combined with a commitment to taxpayer service; and Policy positions and compliance proposals should be sensitive to taxpayer rights and maintain an appropriate balance between enforcement activity and imposition of taxpayer burden.

Achieving greater voluntary compliance and shrinking the tax gap involves a comprehensive, integrated multi-year strategy. Along with increased enforcement activities, components of this strategy also include: reducing opportunities for tax evasion, expanding compliance research, improving information technology, enhancing taxpayer service, reforming and simplifying the tax law and coordinating with partners and stakeholders, such as states and foreign governments, to share compliance strategies. The IRS has made considerable progress in these efforts and will continue taking reasonable steps toward this goal as I will detail later in my testimony.

Chapter 3 – This is the Testimony of J. Russell George, Treasury Inspector General for Tax Administration. Hearing on "Problems at the Internal Revenue Service: Closing the Tax Gap and Preventing Identity Theft."

Chapter 4 – In January 2012, IRS estimated that the gross tax gap—the difference between taxes owed and taxes paid on time—was $450 billion for tax year 2006.

IRS estimated that it would collect $65 billion through enforcement actions and late payments, leaving a net tax gap of $385 billion. From 2001 to 2006, IRS estimated that the gross tax gap increased by $105 billion. However, the percentage of taxes owed that were paid on time remained relatively constant at 83.1 percent in 2006, compared to 83.7 percent in 2001.

Given persistent levels of noncompliance and large and growing structural deficits, it will be important to understand the causes of tax noncompliance and develop new approaches to minimize it.

This testimony addresses two questions: (1) What types of taxpayers are responsible for the tax gap, and what is the nature of their noncompliance? (2) What are strategies for reducing the tax gap? The statement also discusses potential long-term strategies to prevent refund fraud related to identity theft. This statement is based largely on GAO's recent reports and recommendations on tax noncompliance and updates GAO's 2011 testimony on the tax gap.

Chapter 5 – Taxes are necessary because they fund the services provided by government. Several years ago, the Internal Revenue Service (IRS) estimated that the gross tax gap—the difference between taxes owed and taxes paid on time—was $345 billion for 2001. In the face of large and growing deficits, it is important to seek out potential causes and solutions to the tax gap.

Achieving high levels of voluntary compliance is made more challenging as the tax code expands. Tax expenditures—preferential provisions in the code such as exemptions, exclusions, deductions, credits, and deferral of tax liability— have expanded the tax code, more than doubling in number since 1974.

GAO's statement focuses on four key areas: (1) how complexity adds to taxpayer burden and economic efficiency costs; (2) how complexities in reporting income contribute to the tax gap; (3) how tax expenditures add complexity and contribute to the tax gap; and (4) possible strategies for addressing the tax gap. The statement is based largely on GAO's previous work conducted on tax compliance issues affecting individual taxpayers from 2005 through 2011.

Chapter 6 – The Internal Revenue Service (IRS) collects 96 percent of the government's total receipts, approximately $2.7 trillion in FY 2008. The vast majority of those revenues come from taxpayers who voluntarily report and pay the taxes that they owe. The IRS has estimated the overall voluntary compliance rate to be approximately 84 percent.

Despite the voluntary compliance rate and vigorous enforcement by the IRS, a significant amount of revenue remains unreported and unpaid. In 2005, the IRS estimated this gross tax gap to be approximately $345 billion. After subtracting revenue obtained through enforcement actions and other late payments, the IRS estimated the net tax gap to be approximately $290 billion. These estimates, which remain the most recent estimates available, were conducted using data collected in tax year 2001 and before.

As a result of an increase in funding included in the IRS FY 2009 budget, the Department of the Treasury (Treasury) and the IRS have recently initiated intensive efforts to update the estimate of the tax gap on an ongoing basis, which will permit more regular and effective assessments. Consistent with its commitment to long-term fiscal soundness, the Administration is committed to working closely with Congress to narrow the tax gap, which imposes an unfair burden on every American who pays taxes in full. Ongoing updates of the tax gap estimate starting in 2011 will form the basis for regularly assessing progress towards that goal.

Building on reports previously released, this report is intended to provide a comprehensive overview of efforts to close the tax gap. This report is also intended to serve as a baseline for further work and discussion. After briefly discussing the nature and scope of the tax gap, this report summarizes previous Treasury and IRS tax gap reports and identifies the areas of strategic priority detailed in those reports. This report then summarizes the achievements, ongoing efforts, and new initiatives for achieving progress in each of those areas of strategic priority, organized according to the components of the strategy to reduce the tax gap detailed in prior reports.

As this report will make clear, the IRS and Treasury, working with Congress, are pursuing a wide range of initiatives, including a series of legislative proposals included in the Administration's FY 2010 budget. The Administration recognizes the particular value of those efforts and initiatives that improve voluntary compliance by making the tax filing process easier and more taxpayer-friendly. While aggressive enforcement activity can also help to narrow the tax gap, it is important to recognize that increased enforcement efforts require certain trade-offs. The Administration is committed to working closely with Congress to strike an appropriate balance to maximize revenue collection without imposing unreasonable compliance and enforcement burdens on the vast majority of individuals and businesses that fully and willingly pay what they owe.

In: Tax Gaps
Editor: Rondell Meinke
ISBN: 978-1-62417-452-0


*Chapter 1*

# TAX GAP, TAX COMPLIANCE, AND PROPOSED LEGISLATION IN THE 112TH CONGRESS*

*James M. Bickley*

## SUMMARY

Recent and projected large federal budget deficits and the need for revenue offsets under the Pay-As-You-Go Act (PAYGO) have generated congressional interest in the feasibility of increasing revenue by reducing the tax gap. The Internal Revenue Service (IRS) defines the *gross* tax gap as the difference between the tax liability imposed by law for a given tax year and the amount of tax that taxpayers pay *voluntarily* and on time for that year. It defines the *net* tax gap as the amount of the gross tax gap that remains unpaid after all enforced and other late payments are made for the tax year. For tax (calendar) year 2006 (the most recent year for which data are available), the IRS estimated a gross tax gap of $450 billion, equal to a noncompliance rate of 16.9%. For the same tax year, IRS enforcement activities, coupled with other late payments, recovered about $65 billion of the gross tax gap, resulting in an estimated net tax gap of $385 billion.

* This is an edited, reformatted and augmented version of the Congressional Research Service Publication, CRS Report for Congress R42739, dated September 20, 2012.

The estimated gross tax gap of $450 billion consisted of underreporting of tax liability ($376 billion), nonfiling of tax returns ($28 billion), and underpayment of taxes ($46 billion). (Taxes on illegal activities are excluded from these estimates.) Most of the underreporting of tax liability concerned underreporting of individual income liability ($235 billion). The percentage of individual income that was underreported varied significantly depending on the degree of information reporting and whether or not withholding was required. For the 2006 tax gap estimate, the IRS primarily utilized data from the National Research Program (NRP), which seeks to obtain the optimal balance among research quality, efficiency, and the reduction of taxpayer burden. Estimates of the gross tax gap have been heavily publicized; perhaps as a result, some public officials have emphasized better enforcement of tax laws in order to raise revenue. Three factors affect the dollar amount that can be collected by increased enforcement: some types of unreported income are difficult to detect, some of the detected tax liability cannot be easily collected, and many detected tax liabilities are small relative to enforcement costs.

From FY2001 to FY2011, enforcement revenues collected by the IRS increased from $33.8 billion to $55.2 billion. Also from FY2001 to FY2011, IRS staffing for key enforcement occupations rose from 20,203 to 22,184.

Over the past four years, the IRS has focused on six strategy priorities: technology modernization, tax return preparers, data analytics, taxpayer service, offshore tax evasion, and workforce job satisfaction. The pursuit of most of these priorities reduces the tax gap. The IRS has put in place the major facets of its tax return preparer initiative.

In the 112$^{th}$ Congress, legislation concerning tax compliance has been introduced in the following seven areas: repeal of the 1099 reporting requirement (H.R. 4); identity theft (S. 1534, S. 3432, H.R. 3215, H.R. 3482, and H.R. 6205); free file (S. 1796 and H.R. 2569); contracting (H.R. 829); insurance companies (S. 1693 and H.R. 3157); tax havens (S. 1346, H.R. 2669, S. 2075, and H.R. 3338); and tax avoidance by expatriates (S. 3205).

## INTRODUCTION

Recent and projected large federal budget deficits have generated congressional and executive branch interest in increasing revenue by reducing the tax gap.[1] Specific methods for lowering the tax gap may also be used as revenue offsets under the Pay-As-You-Go Act (PAYGO).[2] Other motivations for reducing the tax gap include adverse effects on (1) public trust in the fairness of the tax system, which may adversely affect voluntary compliance with tax laws, and (2) economic efficiency, by providing an incentive for inputs of labor and capital to shift to those sectors of the economy with greater opportunities to evade taxes.[3]

This report defines tax gap concepts, explains the methodology used to estimate the tax gap, discusses the relationship between the tax gap and enforcement, explains the Internal Revenue Service's (IRS's) strategic priorities, examines the IRS return preparer initiative, and describes proposed legislation in the 112$^{th}$ Congress.

## Tax Gap Concepts

The IRS has defined the concepts of a gross tax gap and a net tax gap. The IRS defines the gross tax gap as the difference between the aggregate tax liability imposed by law for a given tax year and the amount of tax that taxpayers pay *voluntarily* and on time for that year.[4] And it defines the *net* tax gap as the amount of the gross tax gap that remains unpaid after all enforced and other late payments are made for the tax year.[5] Also, the net tax gap is measured after any subsequent appeals and litigation; consequently, this measurement is more accurate a number of years after the taxes were due.[6]

Currently, the measurements of these tax gap concepts exclude illegal activities because the IRS lacks adequate data on these activities. Also, the IRS does not currently include the international tax gap. The Treasury Inspector General for Tax Administration has reported that known estimates of the total international tax gap range from a low of $42.8 billion to a high of $123.0 billion.[7] For tax year 2006 (the most recent year for which data are available), the IRS estimated a gross tax gap of $450 billion, equal to a voluntary compliance rate (VCR) of 83.1%.[8] For the same year, IRS enforcement activities, coupled with other late payments, recovered about $65 billion of the gross tax gap, resulting in an estimated net tax gap of $385 billion.[9]

The estimated gross tax gap of $450 billion consisted of underreporting of tax liability ($376 billion), nonfiling of tax returns ($28 billion), and underpayment of taxes ($46 billion).[10] For 2006, the $376 billion of underreporting of tax liability had the following components: $235 billion in individual income tax, $67 billion in corporate income tax, $72 billion in employment tax, and $2 billion in estate taxes.[11] There was no estimate of the underreporting of excise taxes.[12]

The percentage of individual income tax that was underreported varied significantly depending on the degree of information reporting and whether or not withholding was required.[13] For example, in 2006, 1% of the taxes on the sum of wages, salaries, and tips was underreported because of substantial information reporting and withholding.[14] But 56% of the total of nonfarm proprietor income, other income, rents and royalties, farm income, and income on Form 4797 (sales of business property) was underreported due to little or no information reporting.[15] These data indicate that increased information reporting and withholding would reduce the tax gap. The increased revenue would have to be weighed against higher administrative costs of the IRS and higher compliance costs of individuals.

## METHODOLOGY TO ESTIMATE THE TAX GAP

Since taxpayers do not report their underreporting of tax liability, the IRS has utilized evolving methods to estimate the tax gap. Prior to 1989, it used the Taxpayer Compliance Measurement Program (TCMP). Currently, the IRS utilizes the National Research Program (NRP) to estimate the gross income tax gap.[16]

### Taxpayer Compliance Measurement Program

Prior to tax year 1989, the IRS relied on data from the TCMP to estimate the gross tax gap for individual income taxpayers and small corporations (less than $10 million in assets). The IRS formulated upper- and lower-bound estimates of the gross income tax gap. The IRS completed "line-by-line examinations of several different types of tax returns."[17] The upper-bound estimates of the gross tax gap were calculated from the TCMP and regular audits of large corporations. For larger corporations ($10 million or more in assets), the IRS relied on regular operational audits of tax returns. If an audit showed an underpayment of taxes, the IRS examiner determined the tax deficiency.[18]

The lower-bound estimate of the gross tax gap was based on the amounts eventually assessed after the appeals and litigation process. Some of the tax deficiency found from audits was negated by taxpayers' appeals and court decisions leading to a lower estimate of taxes owed but unpaid.[19] "The eventual assessment may be considered to be the true 'legal' liability in the sense that IRS cannot attempt to assess more later, except in unusual cases."[20] The net tax gap differed depending on whether the upper- or lower-bound estimate of the gross tax gap was used.

## National Research Program

The last TCMP was for tax year 1988. Several times in the 1990s, IRS officials attempted to conduct a new TCMP, but some members of Congress objected because of the high cost to the IRS and the compliance burden placed on taxpayers who were selected in the TCMP sample. Consequently, IRS developed the National Research Program. According to the IRS,

> The NRP approach to measuring reporting compliance balances research quality, efficiency and the reduction of taxpayer burden. It establishes a tax return sample that is representative of the individual taxpayer population. NRP focuses on obtaining reliable data in the most cost-effective manner possible by using innovative and efficient techniques that maintain taxpayer rights to privacy.[21]

The NRP was used in estimating the 2001 and 2006 tax gaps. The 2006 tax gap estimates "are based on a variety of data sources and methodologies."[22] The primary source was the NRP for 2006.

> The IRS studied individual taxpayer compliance through the NRP and used the resulting compliance data to estimate the tax gap for individual income tax underreporting and the portion of employment tax underreporting attributed to self-employment taxes for tax year 2006.
>
> The 2006 individual NRP involved auditing a random selection of about 13,000 to 14,000 individual tax returns... . Starting with the 2006 individual NRP compliance study, IRS is using a rolling sample, which will combine samples across three years. According to the IRS, this change will reduce cost and provide more up to date compliance data. The sample design for the 2006 individual NRP included 11 primary strata, which were based on the examination classes used in audit workload selection. Also the 2006 individual NRP was designed to oversample returns with business income reported on Schedules C, E, or F or Form 2106.[23]

# Tax Enforcement

The estimates of the gross tax gap have been heavily publicized. Perhaps as a result, some public officials have emphasized better enforcement of tax laws to increase revenue. According to some, enforcement alone is likely to have a limited impact on the gross tax gap. Acting on this view, the IRS is implementing what it terms a comprehensive approach to reduce the gross tax gap.

## Limitations to Increased Enforcement

Three factors are seen as limiting the net revenue potential from increased enforcement. First, much of the gross tax gap for individual income tax filers is due to types of unreported income that are difficult to detect. Usually the income is not covered by third-party information returns (e.g., income earned by informal business proprietors who operate on a cash basis). Second, even when the unreported income is detected, some of the resulting tax liability cannot be easily collected, particularly from those taxpayers who are currently unable to pay. Third, many detected tax liabilities are so small relative to enforcement costs that it is not seen as cost effective to pursue collection.

## Tax Enforcement Efforts FY2001-FY2011

Some analysts contend that empirical data suggest that additional tax enforcement actions alone would have a limited effect on the gross tax gap.

From FY2001 to FY2011, greater tax enforcement efforts by the IRS increased enforcement revenue from $33.8 billion to $55.2 billion.[24] While $21.4 billion represents a 63.3% increase, it is 6.2% of the estimated $345 billion gross tax gap in 2001. During the period FY2001-FY2007, staffing for key enforcement occupations rose from 20,113 to 21,187 (5.3%); examinations of individual tax returns increased from 731,756 (or 0.58% of returns) to 1,384,563 (or 1.03% of returns); examinations of business returns rose from 7,384,600 (or 0.55% of returns) to 9,072,828 (or 0.66% of returns); and examinations of tax-exempt organization returns increased from 5,342 (or 0.61% of returns) to 7,580 (or 0.87% of returns).[25]

For FY2008, staffing for key enforcement occupations declined to 20,722 from 21,187 in FY2007; the percentage of individual tax returns examined fell to 1.01%; and the percentage of business tax returns examined decreased to 0.63%.[26] For FY2008, the IRS reported a reduction in enforcement revenues to $56.4 billion from $59.2 billion in FY2007.[27] For FY2009, IRS appropriations rose to $11.5 billion and enforcement funding rose to $5.1 billion.[28] For FY2009, staffing for key enforcement occupations rose to 21,059, but enforcement revenue collected declined sharply to $48.9 billion.[29] This amount of revenue collected is only $0.2 billion above the amount collected in FY2006. Mr. Steve Miller, the deputy commissioner for services and enforcement, reportedly said that this decline in revenue collected between FY2008 and FY2009 was due to two factors: the recession and the closing of a significant number of high-grossing tax shelter cases, namely those regarding "Son of Boss" (bond option sales strategy) transactions.[30] The closing of Son of Boss cases also caused a spike in enforcement revenues in FY2007 compared to FY2006.[31] The IRS describes Son of Boss transactions as arrangements that are "designed to produce noneconomic tax losses on the disposition of partnership interests."[32] For FY2010, enforcement revenue collected rebounded to $57.6 billion but declined to $55.2 billion in FY2011. IRS enforcement staffing was 22,710 in FY2010 and 22,184 in FY2011. Taken together those observations suggest that enforcement alone will not effectively close the tax gap.

As a result, rather than focusing only on enforcement, the Treasury Department and the Government Accountability Office (GAO)[33] argued that a comprehensive strategy was needed to reduce the tax gap.

## Comprehensive Strategy for Reducing the Tax Gap

The Office of Tax Policy at the Treasury developed what it considered a comprehensive strategy for reducing the tax gap, guided by the following four key principles:[34]

- Unintentional taxpayer errors and intentional taxpayer evasion should both be addressed.
- Sources of noncompliance should be targeted with specificity.
- Enforcement activities should be combined with a commitment to taxpayer service.
- Policy positions and compliance proposals should be sensitive to taxpayer rights and maintain an appropriate balance between enforcement activity and imposition of taxpayer burden.[35]

Over time, the strategic focus on reducing the tax gap evolved into a broader array of IRS priorities.

## IRS Strategic Priorities

On April 5, 2012, at the National Press Club, IRS Commissioner Douglas H. Shulman explained the six strategy priorities that had been a relentless focus of the IRS over the preceding four years.[36] The IRS's pursuit of most of these priorities reduced the tax gap.

- **Creating New Capabilities and Efficiencies Through Technology**
  Since the 1960s, the IRS had conducted its core account processing on a weekly basis. This processing included basic taxpayer information, such as a taxpayer's current account balance, whether the taxpayer had an outstanding amounts due, and whether the taxpayer made any recent payments. This year the IRS successfully migrated from a weekly processing cycle to daily processing.
  The payoffs from this change are quicker tax return processing for all taxpayers, up-to-date information at the fingertips of IRS's customer account representatives, and a platform for more real-time analytics and compliance.
- **Rethinking and Reimagining the IRS's Relationship with Paid Tax Return Preparers**
  In 2011, 95 million individual and business income tax returns were prepared by paid preparers. The IRS is now well into the process of ensuring a basic competency level for tax return preparers and focusing our enforcement efforts on rooting out unscrupulous preparers. The IRS has registered over 840,000 return preparers and has begun administering a competency test for any preparer who is not a CPA, attorney, or enrolled agent. These individuals also have to complete 15 hours of continuing education each year from IRS-approved providers.[37]
- **Leveraging Data Analytics for Continuous Improvement**
  This IRS has always been an information intensive enterprise. But what matters is the organization of data and ultimately the knowledge and intelligence that IRS extracts from the information. The IRS built a team of people with analytical expertise and connected them with its business units to improve operations continually. They are working on

multiple fronts, and the results have been significant. For example, using better data on return preparers that was gained through IRS's return preparer initiatives and faster processing cycles, the IRS applied advanced data analytics to link tax returns that showed potentially serious compliance issues to the individuals who prepared them. The IRS identified a number of preparers with apparently inaccurate returns and, depending on the type and severity of the issue, is applying different types of compliance tools.

- **Enhancing Taxpayer Service Capabilities**
  Providing quality customer service is a key priority of the IRS. Every year the American Customer Satisfaction Index measures customer satisfaction across various industries and government agencies. This composite index is the main measure used by the IRS to track its overall performance. For 1998, only 32% of respondents voiced satisfaction with IRS service, but this percentage rose to 73% in 2011. Two examples of IRS innovations to improve customer service were e-filing and IRS's Smartphone application called "IRS2Go." In 2011, 77% of individuals used e-filing, which resulted in taxpayers receiving their refunds faster, with fewer data processing errors. The IRS Smartphone application permits taxpayers to check on the status of their refund and obtain other helpful tax information on their iPhones or Androids.
- **Transforming the Agency to Confront the Challenges of a Global Economy**
  In a world where products are routinely sold after intellectual property is generated in one or more countries ... where logistics and engineering are carried out in other counties ... where risks are managed in a variety of places ... and where components are sourced from multiple jurisdictions, figuring out what U.S. corporate income tax may be appropriate when the products go to market can be a challenge to say the least. For individuals, the IRS views the reduction of offshore tax evasion as an issue of fundamental fairness. Over the past four years, the IRS significantly increased its resources and focus on offshore tax evasion, and the results have been substantial. In 2009, the IRS gave taxpayers, involved in offshore tax evasion, a chance to come in voluntarily and avoid going to jail. At the end of 2011, approximately 33,000 individuals had voluntarily disclosed their unpaid offshore taxes, and consequently, paid more than $4.4 billion in back taxes and penalties. The IRS is moving from

information sharing to more coordinated action among government tax authorities on a global basis. The Commissioner of the IRS is the chairman of the main global body of tax authorities, which comprises his counterparts from 43 nations, including those from all G20 nations.[38]

- **Positioning the IRS Workforce to Prepare for Tomorrow's Challenges**
  The IRS initiated the "Workforce of Tomorrow Task Force" with the stated purpose objective of making the IRS the best place to work in government. The IRS put an emphasis on key factors including engagement, accountability, career paths, and management to position the agency for excellence in the future. From 2008 to 2011, the IRS jumped from eighth to third place among the fifteen large agencies with over 20,000 employees in the survey of the "Best Place to Work in the Federal Government."

Following IRS Commissioner Shulman's annual speech, much of the question-and- answer period focused on IRS's return preparer initiative.[39]

## IRS Return Preparer Initiative

In June 2009, the IRS began a review of tax return preparers and obtained extensive feedback from a diverse community of stakeholders.[40] The IRS had the authority to establish regulations regarding tax return preparers without legislative approval. After a review of return preparers, the IRS established a return preparer initiative with new regulations, which it began implementing in 2010.[41]

On June 5, 2012, the IRS marked the third anniversary of it return preparer initiative and indicated that major facets of the initiative were now in place.[42] The IRS published the following initiative highlights:[43]

- **Mandatory Registration and Use of a Preparer Tax Identification Number(PTIN):** Anyone who is paid to prepare, or help prepare, all or substantially all of a federal tax return now has to register with the IRS and obtain a PTIN, as do all enrolled agents. The PTIN is valid for a calendar year and must be renewed annually. Almost 850,000 preparers have registered since the requirement began.

- **Competency Test:** In November 2011, a 120-question basic competency test was launched. Certain preparers are required to take the test by December 31, 2013, to stay in business. The IRS urges an estimated 340,000 preparers required to take the test to do so as soon as possible to give themselves more time if they have to retake the test and to avoid a potential flood of last-minute test takers. Certified Public Accountants (CPAs), Enrolled Agents (EAs), and attorneys are exempt from the test because they already have other testing requirements as part of their credentials. Certain non-signing preparers supervised by CPAs, EAs, or attorneys are exempt, as are non-1040 preparers.
- **Continuing Education (CE):** The roughly 340,000 preparers who have a testing requirement also have a new requirement to complete 15 hours of continuing education courses each year. The CE credits must include 10 hours in federal tax law, three hours in federal tax law changes, and two hours in ethics. This requirement became effective January 2012 and it applies even if the preparer has not yet taken the test. There are now hundreds of outlets offering IRS-approved CE courses. More details are available at http://www.irs.gov/taxpros/ce.
- **Ethics and Tax Compliance:** Ethical requirements that previously applied only to CPAs, EAs, and attorneys now apply to all paid return preparers. All paid preparers also will undergo a tax compliance check and are subject to the standards for practice outlined in Treasury Department Circular 230.
- **Registered Tax Return Preparer (RTRP):** Preparers who pass the competency test and tax compliance check are given a new credential: Registered Tax Return Preparer. To date, over 4,800 people have become Registered Tax Return Preparers. Beginning in 2014, only Registered Tax Return Preparers, Enrolled Agents, Certified Public Accountants, and attorneys will be authorized to prepare individual income tax returns for compensation.
- **Public Database:** The IRS also will create a publicly searchable database that will allow taxpayers to see if their tax preparers have met IRS standards or to find a tax preparer in their zip code area. The IRS will have a public education campaign to inform taxpayers to use only CPAs, EAs, attorneys, or Registered Tax Return Preparers if they pay to have their taxes prepared. The database will also show any credentials held by the preparer, including the new RTRP credential,

as well as those who are EAs, CPAs, and attorneys. The RTRP competency test is available at more than 260 vendor testing centers nationwide. Preparers can determine if they have a test requirement by going to their online PTIN Account at http://www.irs.gov/tin. Preparers also can set a test date, time and location through their online PTIN Account.

# PROPOSED LEGISLATION IN THE 112TH CONGRESS

In the 112th Congress, numerous bills have been proposed concerning the tax gap and tax compliance. All of these bills were referred to committee, and one has become public law. These bills are categorized into seven categories and described in the following sections.[44]

## Repeal of 1099 Reporting Requirement

***P.L. 112-9, (H.R. 4). Comprehensive 1099 Taxpayer Protection and Repayment of Exchange Subsidy Overpayments Act of 2011***

On January 12, 2011, Representative Daniel E. Lungren introduced H.R. 4. On April 14, 2011, this bill became P.L. 112-9. Because the bill was enacted, the related bills (H.Res. 129, H.R. 60, H.R. 144, H.R. 584, H.R. 705, S. 18, S. 72, S. 359) are not described in this report. This public law amended the Internal Revenue Code to (1) repeal requirements for the reporting to the IRS of payments of $600 or more to corporations that are not tax-exempt and of gross proceeds of $600 or more paid in consideration for any type of property; (2) repeal requirements for reporting payments made with respect to rental property which is not part of a trade or business; and (3) increase, for taxable years ending after December 31, 2013, the advance applicable dollar amount of the tax credit for health care premium assistance for taxpayers whose household income is less the 400% of the poverty line.[45]

## Identity Theft

Five bills were introduced concerning identify theft: H.R. 3215, H.R. 3338, H.R. 3482, H.R. 6205, S. 1534, and S. 3432.

### *S. 1534, S. 3432, and H.R. 3215—Identify Theft and Tax Fraud Prevention Act*

On September 8, 2011, Senator Bill Nelson introduced S. 1534. On July 25, 2012, Senator Nelson introduced S. 3432. On October 14, 2011, Representative Kathy Castor introduced H.R. 3215. S. 1534, S. 3432, and H.R. 3215 are related bills. The bills would amend the Internal Revenue Code to (1) impose a fine and/or prison term on any person who knowingly or willfully misappropriates another person's tax identification number in connection with any list, return, account, statement, or other documents submitted to the IRS; (2) increase the civil and criminal penalties for improper disclosure or use of taxpayer information by tax return preparers; (3) require the Commissioner of Internal Revenue to submit to the Senate Committee on Finance and the House Committee on Ways and Means an annual report on the number of reported cases of tax fraud and suspected tax fraud and the actions taken in response to such reports; and (4) require the head of the Federal Bureau of Prisons to submit to Congress a detailed plan on how it will use tax information provided by the IRS to reduce prison tax fraud. The bills would direct the Secretary of the Treasury to (1) implement an identity theft tax fraud prevention program; and (2) review whether current federal tax law prevents the effective enforcement of local, state, and federal identity theft statutes. The bills would authorize the IRS Commissioner to transfer appropriated funds to be used solely to prevent and resolve potential tax fraud cases. The bills would direct the Commissioner to establish in the Criminal Investigation Division of the IRS the position of Local Law Enforcement Liaison to coordinate the investigation of tax fraud with state and local law enforcement agencies and communicate the status of tax fraud cases involving identity theft. The bills would direct the Comptroller General to study and report on the role of prepaid debit cards and commercial tax preparation software in facilitating fraudulent tax returns through identity theft. The bills would prohibit the Secretary of Commerce from disclosing information contained in the Death Master File relating to deceased individual to persons who are not certified to access such information.[46] S. 3432 differs from the other two bills in that it includes a section titled "Prohibiting the Display of Social Security Account Numbers on Newly Issued Medicare Identification Cards and Communications Provided to Medicare Beneficiaries."

### *H.R. 3482—Tax Crimes and Identity Theft Prevention Act*

On December 2, 2011, Representative Kathy Castor introduced H.R. 3482, which is related to S. 1534 and H.R. 3215. The only addition to the preceding summary on S. 1534/S. 3215 is a section that authorizes the Attorney General to award grants to state and local law enforcement agencies for the investigation and prosecution of tax crimes.

### *H.R. 6205—Protect and Save Act of 2012*

On July 26, 2012, Representative Richard Nugent introduced H.R. 6205.[47]

The bill would authorize the Secretary of the Treasury to disclose income tax return information to officers and employees of any federal law enforcement agency, or any officers and employees of any state or local law enforcement agency, who are personally and directly engaged in the investigation of any crimes pertaining to the misuse of the identity of another person for purposes of filing a false or fraudulent tax return, upon receipt of a written request. This request must be made by the head of the agency (or his delegate) involved in the investigation, and the request must set forth the specific reason why such disclosure may be relevant to the investigation. The bill would require the Commissioner of the IRS to establish within the Criminal Investigation Division the position of Local Law Enforcement Liaison. The bill would also require the Secretary of the Treasury (or the Secretary's delegate) to implement an identify theft fraud prevention program.

The bill would require the Comptroller General to conduct a study on the use of prepaid debit cards and commercial tax preparation software in tax fraud. The bill would also require the Comptroller General to study the use of e-filing in tax fraud. The bill would extend the authority of the IRS to disclose certain tax return information to prison officials. The bill would restrict the Secretary of Commerce in disclosing information contained in the Social Security Death Master File with respect to any individual who had died during the previous two calendar years.

## Free File

### *S. 1796 and H.R. 2569—Free File Program Act of 2011*

On November 3, 2011, Senator Mark L. Pryor introduced S. 1796. On July 15, 2011, Representative Peter J. Roskam introduced H.R. 2569. S. 1796 and H.R. 2569 are related bills. These bills authorize and direct the Secretary of the Treasury to continue to implement and operate the Internal Revenue Service's Free File program (free online individual income tax preparation and electronic filing services provided by the private sector technology industry to lower-income taxpayers).

## Contracting

***H.R. 829—Contracting and Tax Accountability Act of 2011***

On February 28, 2011, Representative Jason Chaffetz introduced H.R. 829. This bill would prohibit any person who has a seriously delinquent tax debt from obtaining a federal government contract or grant. The bill would require federal agency heads to require prospective recipients of a contract or grant in excess of an amount equal to the simplified acquisition threshold to (1) certify that they do not have such a debt; and (2) authorize the Secretary of the Treasury to disclose information describing whether they have such a debt.

The bill would define "seriously delinquent tax debt" as an outstanding tax debt for which a notice of lien has been filed in public records.

## Insurance Companies

***S. 1693 and H.R. 3157—A Bill to Amend the Internal Revenue Code of 1986 to Prevent the Avoidance of Tax by Insurance Companies through Reinsurance with Non-taxed Affiliates***

On October 12, 2011, Senator Robert Menendez introduced S. 1693. On October 12, 2011, Representative Richard E. Neal introduced H.S. 3157. S. 1693 and H.R. 3157 are related bills. These bills would amend the Internal Revenue Code to exclude from the taxable income of a life insurance company or other insurance company (1) any non-taxed reinsurance premium; (2) any additional amount paid by an insurance company with respect to the reinsurance for which such non-taxed reinsurance premium is paid; and (3) any return premium, ceding commission, reinsurance recovered, or other amount received by an insurance company with respect to the reinsurance for which such non-taxed reinsurance premium is paid.

## Tax Havens[48]

In the 112$^{th}$ Congress, four bills concerning tax havens have been introduced: S. 1346, H.R. 2669, H.R. 3338, and S. 2075.

***S. 1346 and H.R. 2669—Stop Tax Haven Abuse Act***

On July 12, 2011, Senator Carl Levin introduced S. 1346. On July 27, 2011, Representative Lloyd Doggett introduced H.R. 2669. S. 1346 and H.R. 2699 are related bills.

These bills would authorize the Secretary of the Treasury to impose restrictions on foreign jurisdictions or financial institutions operating in the United States that are of prime money laundering concern or that impede U.S. tax enforcement.

The bills would amend the Internal Revenue Code to (1) establish a rebuttable presumption against the validity of transactions by institutions that do not comply with reporting requirements under the Foreign Account Tax Compliance Act (FATCA); (2) treat certain foreign corporations managed and controlled primarily in the United States as domestic corporations for tax purposes; (3) require tax withholding agents and financial institutions to report certain information about beneficial owners of foreign-owned financial accounts; (4) treat credit default swap payments sent offshore as taxable U.S. source income; (5) allow the use of tax return information to evaluate foreign financial account reports; (6) increase penalties for promoting abusive tax shelters and for aiding and abetting the understatement of tax liability; (7) prohibit tax advisor contingent fee agreements for obtaining a tax savings or benefit; and (8) impose additional requirements for third-party summonses used to obtain information in tax investigations that do not identify the person with respect to whose liability the summons is issued.

The bills would amend the Securities Exchange Act of 1934 to (1) require corporations registered with the Securities and Exchange Commission (SEC) to report annually, on a country-by-country basis, on employees' sales, financing, tax obligations, and tax payments; and (2) authorize a fine of up to $1 million for failure to disclose any holding or transaction involving equity or debt instruments known to involve a foreign entity that would otherwise be subject to disclosure requirements. The bills would require the Treasury Secretary to publish a proposed rule in the *Federal Register* requiring unregistered investment companies, including hedge funds or private equity funds, to establish anti-money laundering programs and submit suspicious activity reports. The bills would extend anti-money laundering requirements to persons engaged in the business of forming new businesses or other legal entities. The bills would require federal banking agencies and the SEC to develop examination techniques to detect and prevent abusive tax shelter activities or the aiding or abetting of tax evasion by financial institutions.

The bills would require the Treasury Secretary to (1) disclose tax return information to federal financial regulators for purposes of tax-shelter investigations; (2) disclose to Congress documents relating to a determination to grant, deny, revoke, or restore the tax-exempt status of an organization; and

(3) expand the standards applicable to tax practitioners for issuing written advice on transactions which have a potential for tax avoidance or evasion.

***S. 2075—CUT Loopholes Act or Cut Unjustified Tax Loopholes Act***

On February 7, 2012, Senator Carl Levin introduced S. 2075, which is related to S. 1346 and H.R. 2669. The significant difference is that S. 2075 would curtail tax advantages for stock options.[49]

***H.R. 3338—Stop Outsourcing and Create American Jobs Act of 2011***

On November 3, 2011, Representative Jerry McNerney introduced H.R. 3338. The bill would direct the Secretary of the Treasury to develop and publish a list of countries that are tax havens for corporations. The bill would amend the Internal Revenue Code to increase the penalties on corporations for (1) underpayment of tax involving an undisclosed foreign asset located in a tax-haven country; (2) reportable transaction understatements involving transactions in a tax-haven country; and (3) fraud, tax evasion, or false statements involving transactions in a tax-haven country. The bill would require revenues generated by the act to be set aside for the reduction of the public debt.

## Tax Avoidance by Expatriates

***S. 3205—Ex-PATRIOT Act or Expatriation Prevention by Abolishing Tax-Related Incentives for Offshore Tenancy Act***

On May 17, 2012, Senator Charles E. Schumer introduced S. 3205. This bill would amend the Internal Revenue Code to impose a 30% tax and withholding on capital gains income realized by a nonresident alien individual present in the United States for periods aggregating to 183 days or more or an expatriate who has renounced his or her U.S. citizenship for tax avoidance purposes (specified expatriate). This bill would amend the Immigration and Nationality Act to (1) render a specified expatriate inadmissible to the United State; and (2) prohibit any waiver of such inadmissibility. The bill would direct the Secretary of the Treasury, in consultation with the Secretaries of State and Homeland Security, to develop a policy for granting a waiver of inadmissibility to a specified expatriate who satisfies a tax liability related to such expatriate's renunciation of U.S. citizenship.

# APPENDIX A. TAX GAP DATA FOR 2006

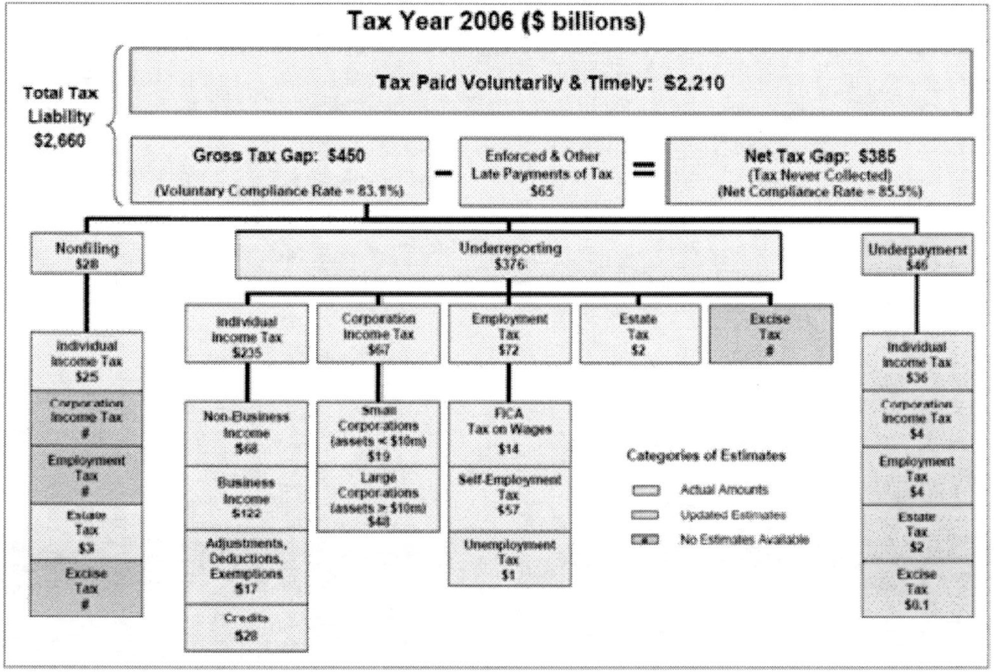


Source: U.S. Treasury, Internal Revenue Service, December 2011.

Figure A-1.Tax Year 2006.

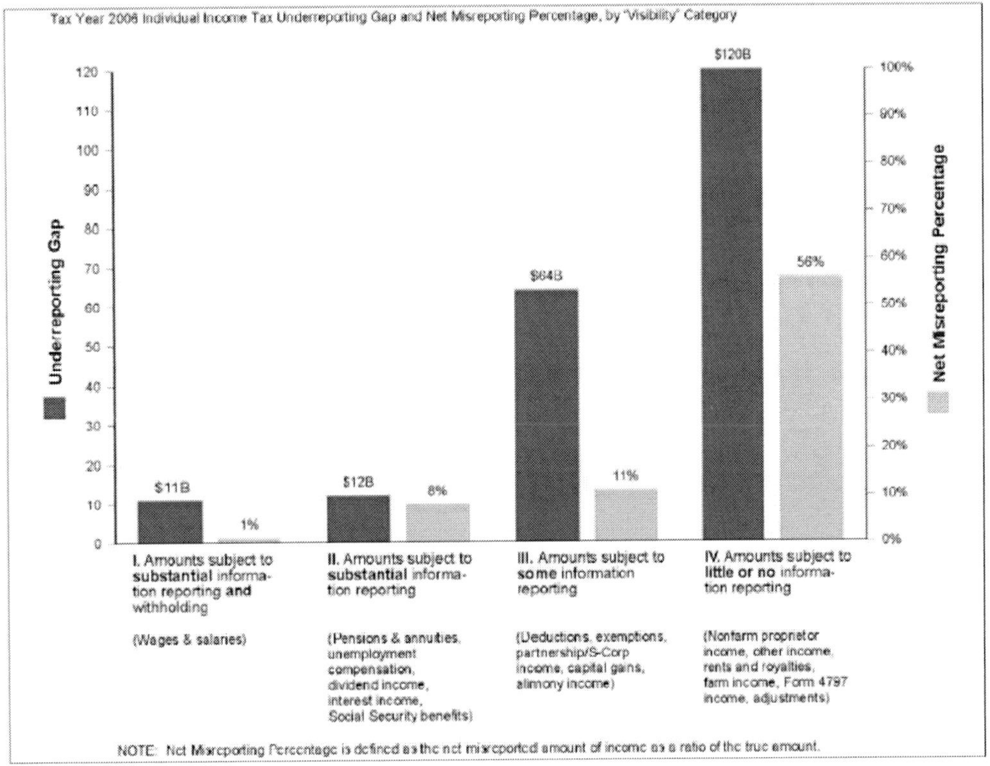


Source: U.S. Treasury, Internal Revenue Service, December 2011.

Figure A-2. Effect of Information Reporting on Taxpayer Compliance, 2006.

# APPENDIX B. IRS ENFORCEMENT RESULTS

**Table B-1. Enforcement Revenues Collected, FY2001-FY2011 (billions of dollars)**

| | FY2001 | FY2002 | FY2003 | FY2004 | FY2005 | FY2006 | FY2007 | FY2008 | FY2009 | FY2010 | FY2011 |
|---|---|---|---|---|---|---|---|---|---|---|---|
| Collection[a] | $24.3 | $24.4 | $24.8 | $25.7 | $26.6 | $28.2 | $31.8 | $31.1 | $26.9 | $29.1 | $31.1 |
| Examination | $7.9 | $7.9 | $10.7 | $14.7 | $17.7 | $17.2 | $23.5 | $20.6 | $17.4 | $16.9 | $12.4 |
| Appeals[b] | $2.3 | $2.2 | $1.9 | $2.2 | $3.9 | $4.3 | $8.3 | $4.8 | $4.8 | $6.7 | $6.5 |
| Documentation Matching | $1.6 | $1.8 | $2.2 | $2.7 | $3.1 | $3.3 | $3.9 | $4.7 | $4.6 | $4.9 | $5.2 |
| **Total[c]** | **$33.8** | **$34.1** | **$37.6** | **$43.1** | **$47.3** | **$48.7** | **$59.2** | **$56.4** | **$48.9** | **$57.6** | **$55.2** |

Source: U.S. Department of the Treasury, Internal Revenue Service, 2011.

a. Enforcement revenue collected in a fiscal year includes tax, interest, and penalties from multiple years.

b. Includes any revenue collection attributable to IRS appeals activities.

c. Totals include revenues from the Information Reporter Program (IRP) and the Automated Underreporter (AUR) Program.

### Table B-2. Staffing for Key Enforcement Occupations, FY2001-FY2011

| | FY2001 | FY2002 | FY2003 | FY2004 | FY2005 | FY2006 | FY2007 | FY2008 | FY2009 | FY2010 | FY2011 |
|---|---|---|---|---|---|---|---|---|---|---|---|
| Revenue Officers[a] | 5,376 | 5,502 | 5,076 | 5,156 | 5,249 | 5,627 | 5,662 | 5,492 | 5,451 | 6,042 | 5,619 |
| Revenue Agents | 12,092 | 11,743 | 11,780 | 11,811 | 12,192 | 12,778 | 12,816 | 12,599 | 12,958 | 13,888 | 13,867 |
| Special Agents | 2,735 | 2,868 | 2,834 | 2,778 | 2,771 | 2,780 | 2,709 | 2,631 | 2,650 | 2,780 | 2,698 |
| **Total** | **20,203** | **20,113** | **19,691** | **19,746** | **20,211** | **21,185** | **21,187** | **20,722** | **21,059** | **22,710** | **22,184** |

Source: U.S. Department of the Treasury, Internal Revenue Service, 2011.

a. Enforcement staffing levels presented in full time equivalents (FTEs). FTEs funded directly by the enforcement appropriation and by reimbursements are included.

## End Notes

[1] For the current outlook on the federal budget, see U.S. Congressional Budget Office, *An Update to the Budget and Economic Outlook: Fiscal Years 2012 to 2022*, August 2012.

[2] For information about PAYGO, see CRS Report R41157, *The Statutory Pay-As-You-Go Act of 2010: Summary and Legislative History*, by Bill Heniff Jr.

[3] For a comprehensive review of the literature on tax compliance, see James Adreoni, Brian Erard, and Jonathan Feinstein, "Tax Compliance," *Journal of Economic Literature*, vol. 36, no. 2, June 1998, pp. 818-860. For an overview of the economics of tax evasion, see Joel Slemrod, "Cheating Ourselves: The Economics of Tax Evasion," *Journal of Economic Perspectives*, vol. 21, no. 1, winter 2007, pp. 25-48.

[4] U.S. Department of the Treasury, Internal Revenue Service, *Reducing the Federal Tax Gap: A Report on Improving Voluntary Compliance*, August 2, 2007, p. 6.

[5] Ibid., pp. 9-10.

[6] U.S. General Accounting Office, *Taxpayer Compliance: Analyzing the Nature of the Income Tax Gap*, Statement of Lynda D. Willis, Director, Tax Policy and Administration Issues, General Government Division, before the National Commission on Restructuring the Internal Revenue Service, GAO/T-GGD-97-35, January 9, 1997, p. 3.

[7] U.S. Department of the Treasury, Treasury Inspector General for Tax Administration, *A Combination of Legislative Actions and Increased IRS Capacity are Required to Reduce the Multi-Billion Dollar U.S. International Tax Gap*, report reference number 2009-IE-R001, January 27, 2009, p. 19.

[8] The VCR is defined as 1 minus the ratio of the gross tax gap to total liabilities. U.S. Department of the Treasury, Internal Revenue Service, *Tax Gap for Tax Year 2006: Overview*, January 6, 2012, p. 1.

[9] U. S. Department of the Treasury, Internal Revenue Service, *Tax Gap "Map,"* December 2011.This reference is shown in **Figure A-1** in **Appendix A**.

[10] Ibid.

[11] Ibid.

[12] Ibid.

[13] U.S. Department of the Treasury, Internal Revenue Service, *Effect of Information Reporting on Taxpayer Compliance,* 2006, December 2011. This reference is shown in **Figure A-2** in **Appendix A**.

[14] Ibid.

[15] Ibid.

[16] These methodologies to estimate the tax gap are examined in detail in the following source: Eric Toder, "What is the Tax Gap?" *Tax Notes*, October 22, 2007, pp. 367-388.

[17] Internal Revenue Service, *Income Tax Compliance Research: Net Tax Gap and Remittance Gap Estimates* (Washington, April 1990), p. 2.

[18] Ibid., p. 13.

[19] Ibid., pp. 13-14.

[20] Ibid., p. 14.

[21] U.S. Treasury, Internal Revenue Service, *Internal Revenue Service Manual – NRP Overview*, Chapter 22, Section 1, April 25, 2008.

[22] U.S. Government Accountability Office, *Tax Gap: Sources of Noncompliance and Strategies to Reduce It*, Statement of James R. White, Director Strategic Issues, before the U.S. Congress, House Committee on Oversight and Government Reform, GAO-12-651T, April 19, 2012, p. 16.

[23] Ibid.

[24] U.S. Department of the Treasury, Internal Revenue Service, *Fiscal Year 2011 Enforcement Results*, p. 1.

[25] Ibid., pp. 2-6.

[26] Ibid., pp. 1-4.

[27] **Appendix B** contains data on IRS enforcement revenues collected and staffing for key enforcement occupations for FY2001-FY2011.

[28] Office of Management and Budget, *Budget of the U.S. Government, Fiscal Year 2011* (Washington: GPO, 2010), p. 115.

[29] U.S. Treasury, Internal Revenue Service, *Fiscal Year 2011 Enforcement Results*, p. 1.

[30] Lauren Gardner, "IRS FY 2009 Enforcement Data Show Impact of Drop in Enforcement Revenue," *Daily Tax Report*, no. 244, December 23, 2009, p. G5.

[31] Ibid.

[32] U.S. Department of the Treasury, Treasury Inspector General for Tax Administration, *Despite the Success Achieved, the Son of Boss Settlement Had Little Impact on Investor Filing and Payment Compliance*, reference number 2009-30-018, December 30, 2008, p. 1.

[33] U.S. Government Accountability Office, *Tax Compliance: Multiple Approaches Are Needed to Reduce the Tax Gap,* Statement of Michael Brostek, Director, Tax Issues Strategic Issues Team, before U.S. Congress, Senate Committee on the Budget, January 23, 2007.

[34] U.S. Department of the Treasury, Office of Tax Policy, *A Comprehensive Strategy for Reducing the Tax Gap,* September 26, 2006. This report was updated with more detailed information about the tax gap and components of the strategy to reduce the tax gap. This updated report is U.S. Department of the Treasury, Internal Revenue Service, *Reducing the Federal Tax Gap, Report on Improving Voluntary Compliance*, August 2, 2007. On July 8, 2009, a second update was issued by the U.S. Treasury, *Update on Reducing the Federal Tax Gap and Improving Voluntary Compliance.*

[35] U.S. Department of the Treasury, Office of Tax Policy, *A Comprehensive Strategy for Reducing the Tax Gap*, pp. 1-2.

[36] U.S. Department of the Treasury, Internal Revenue Service, News Release (IR-2012-42), *Prepared Remarks of Commissioner of Internal Revenue*, April 15, 2012. The following six bulleted entries are a mix of direct or slightly edited quotes from his prepared remarks.

[37] This initiative is examined in detail in the next section of this report.

[38] The G20 includes 19 country members and the European Union, which together represent around 90% of Global GDP, 80% of global trade, and two-thirds of the world's population. The G20 is a forum for international cooperation on important aspects of the international economic and financial agenda. This description is from the following G20 website: http://www.g20.org/index.php/en/what-is-the-g20.

[39] Rachel Boehm, "Shulman to Step Down in November; IRS Priorities Include Extenders, Preparers," *Daily Tax Report*, April 6, 2012, p. G2.

[40] U.S. Department of the Treasury, Internal Revenue Service, *Return Preparer Review*, Publication 4832, December 2009, p. 1.

[41] Ibid., pp. 3-5.

[42] U.S. Department of the Treasury, Internal Revenue Service, "IRS Marks Third Anniversary of Return Preparer Review; Urges Required Preparers to Take Competency Test as Soon as Possible," IRS New Release (IR-2012-59), June 5, 2012, p. 1.

[43] The following bulleted entries are mix of direct or slightly edited quotes from U.S. Department of the Treasury, Internal Revenue Service, "IRS Marks Third Anniversary of Return Preparer Review," pp. 1-2.

[44] Unless indicated otherwise, these descriptions are quotes or paraphrases from the CRS Legislative Information System data base.

[45] For more information, see CRS Report R41782, *1099 Information Reporting Requirements and Penalties: Recent Legislative Activity*, by Carol A. Pettit and Edward C. Liu.

[46] The Social Security Death Master File is a database used by leading government, financial investigative, and credit reporting organizations and medical research and other industries to verify death as well as to prevent fraud. This information is from the U.S. Department of Commerce, National Technical Information Service, at http://www.ntis.gov/products/ssa-dmf.aspx.

[47] This description was written by the author.

[48] For an analysis of tax havens, see CRS Report R40623, *Tax Havens: International Tax Avoidance and Evasion*, by Jane G. Gravelle.

[49] For an explanation of the taxation of employee stock options, see CRS Report RL31458, *Employee Stock Options: Tax Treatment and Tax Issues*, by James M. Bickley.

In: Tax Gaps
Editor: Rondell Meinke
ISBN: 978-1-62417-452-0


*Chapter 2*

# TESTIMONY OF STEVEN T. MILLER, DEPUTY COMMISSIONER FOR SERVICES AND ENFORCEMENT, INTERNAL REVENUE SERVICE. HEARING ON "PROBLEMS AT THE INTERNAL REVENUE SERVICE: CLOSING THE TAX GAP AND PREVENTING IDENTITY THEFT"*

## INTRODUCTION AND SUMMARY

Chairman Platts, Ranking Member Towns and Members of the Subcommittee on Government Organization, Efficiency and Financial Management, my name is Steven Miller and I am the Deputy Commissioner for Services and Enforcement at the Internal Revenue Service. I appreciate the opportunity to testify on the important issue of the tax gap, and discuss actions that the IRS is taking to improve voluntary compliance with our nation's tax laws.

The tax gap is the difference between the amount of tax imposed on taxpayers for a given year and the amount that is paid voluntarily and timely. The tax gap represents, in dollar terms, the annual amount of noncompliance

---

* This is an edited, reformatted and augmented version of the testimony given on April 19, 2012 before the House Committee on Oversight and Government Reform, Subcommittee on Government Organization, Efficiency and Financial Management.

with our tax laws. While no system can ever achieve 100 percent compliance, the IRS has been and remains committed to finding ways to increase compliance.

The IRS recently released an updated tax gap study covering the tax year 2006 which shows that the nation's compliance rate for that year of 83.1 percent is essentially unchanged from the last review covering tax year 2001. The report also showed that the net tax gap in dollars for 2006 was $385 billion.

In terms of what makes up the tax gap, the underreporting of business income by individual taxpayers – income of sole proprietors, farmers and those earning rental, royalty, partnership and S Corporation income – is the largest contributor, accounting for $122 billion of the total in 2006. That is because this income, for which little or no reporting is required for income tax purposes, is the least adequately reported.

We at the IRS are often asked what actions we are taking to close the tax gap. I include in my testimony a number of initiatives, from providing taxpayer services to individuals and businesses grappling with a complex tax code, to running targeted compliance and enforcement programs to address a wide variety of compliance issues. But it is important to understand that while the tax gap is a helpful guide to the scale of tax compliance in the economy, it greatly overstates the amount of deficit reduction that could be achieved through IRS enforcement alone. In other words, it is unrealistic to imagine that IRS enforcement revenues, which stood at $55.2 billion for FY 2011, could grow to a level that would close the net tax gap ($385 billion). Further, major attempts to close the gap must be considered within a context that considers taxpayer burden and taxpayer rights.

At the same time, targeted investments in IRS enforcement such as those included in the Administration's FY 2013 budget request have a high return on investment and serve to improve overall compliance. Steady increases in enforcement resources applied to well-founded examination and collection programs, coupled with increases in selected third-party reporting requirements, are proven cost-effective means of reducing the tax gap.

We also should not lose sight of the fact that failures to comply with tax law often involve unintentional mistakes that are the result of not fully understanding what has come to be an extremely complex tax code. For that reason, a truly comprehensive strategy to increase tax compliance must also include programs to educate taxpayers in their tax obligations and efforts at improving customer service, to make it easier for individuals and businesses to fulfill filing requirements.

In its efforts to address the tax gap and improve tax compliance, the IRS follows four guiding principles:

- Both unintentional taxpayer errors and intentional taxpayer evasion should be addressed;
- Sources of noncompliance should be targeted with specificity;
- Enforcement activities should be combined with a commitment to taxpayer service; and
- Policy positions and compliance proposals should be sensitive to taxpayer rights and maintain an appropriate balance between enforcement activity and imposition of taxpayer burden.

Achieving greater voluntary compliance and shrinking the tax gap involves a comprehensive, integrated multi-year strategy. Along with increased enforcement activities, components of this strategy also include: reducing opportunities for tax evasion, expanding compliance research, improving information technology, enhancing taxpayer service, reforming and simplifying the tax law and coordinating with partners and stakeholders, such as states and foreign governments, to share compliance strategies.

The IRS has made considerable progress in these efforts and will continue taking reasonable steps toward this goal as I will detail later in my testimony.

## MEASURING THE TAX GAP

The tax gap statistic is a helpful guide to the scale of tax compliance and to the persisting sources of low compliance but it is not an adequate guide to year-to-year changes. The statistic is also useful in providing the big picture of the relationship between tax liability on the books and tax receipts available to support Federal Government activity, but it should be viewed in the context of a broad range of compliance studies, some of which analyze specific initiatives designed to increase tax compliance.

The tax gap can be viewed in two different ways. There is the gross tax gap, which is simply the amount of true tax liability faced by taxpayers that is not paid on time. For 2006 it is estimated to be $450 billion. The net tax gap of $385 billion represents the amount of true tax liability that is not only not paid on time but is also not collected subsequently, either voluntarily or as the result of enforcement activities. Thus, the net tax gap represents the amount of tax liability that is never paid.

The gross and net tax gap estimates provide only a small portion of the information produced under the tax gap rubric at the IRS. Component tax gap estimates, distinguishing unpaid tax liability by mode of compliance, by tax source and by income source, provide a "map" of where noncompliance is concentrated. Further breakouts, some for specific tax return line items, add additional information.

## Components of the Tax Gap

When looked at by mode of compliance, the tax gap can be divided into three components: Nonfiling, or not filing required returns on time; underreporting, or not reporting one's full tax liability when the return is filed on time; and underpayment, or not paying by the due date the full amount of tax reported on a timely filed return. Underreporting constitutes 84 percent of the tax gap for 2006, while underpayment constitutes 10 percent and nonfiling 6 percent.

The underpayment gap is calculated directly from IRS administrative records for the individual income tax, the corporate income tax, employment taxes, the estate tax and excise taxes. Taxpayers who have filed returns indicating taxes owed but who have not paid the full amounts on time are identified upon filing. The difference between taxes owed as reported on returns and the amounts paid on time is the underpayment gap.

The other two components of the tax gap – nonfiling and underreporting – present vastly greater estimation challenges because they measure activity that is either not revealed to the IRS at all (e.g. failure to file a return) or is reported in understated or otherwise mischaracterized fashion. Estimating those components of the tax gap entails two logical steps: estimating how many taxpayers engage in noncompliant activity and estimating the tax liabilities that they incur but do not report. Those two steps are combined in different ways to estimate the nonfiling and the underreporting gaps.

For example, the figure for the individual income tax nonfiling gap in 2006 was developed using IRS administrative data to identify taxpayers who appeared on a return filed late and taxpayers who did not appear on a return at all. The estimate associated with late returns began with the balance due reported on those returns, but also took into account additional income reported on third-party information documents. The tax on those updated returns was then estimated using a tax calculator. The estimate associated with people who did not file any return followed a similar procedure that also relied on income and withholding reported on third-party information documents.

The predominant method used to calculate the underreporting gap involves auditing a statistically selected sample of taxpayers. Research audits are time consuming, but they constitute the only viable method for estimating the underreporting gap for the individual income tax. This program, called the National Research Program (NRP), has been in place since 2000. The information gleaned from these audits helps examiners more effectively select the types of cases to audit, and offers other detailed insights about noncompliant behavior used throughout the IRS to better target service and enforcement work. The NRP uses random audits for the underreporting gap and compiles data for the underpayment gap, which is tabulated from the Master File. The NRP office is also involved in nonfiling estimation efforts.

### Importance of Information Reporting

One of the key findings from our research on the tax gap has been that tax compliance is far higher when reported amounts are subject to information reporting and, more so, when subject to withholding as well. For 2006, the net misreporting percentage (NMP) – taking the net amount that was misreported and expressing it as a ratio of the true amount – is 1 percent for amounts subject to substantial information reporting and withholding, and 8 percent for amounts subject to substantial information reporting without withholding. But the NMP jumps to 56 percent for amounts, such as business income, that are subject to little or no information reporting or withholding. These statistics provide further confirmation that "visibility" of income sources and financial transactions is the main factor in high compliance rates, and information reporting is one of the few means of sizably increasing the compliance rate. Therefore, it is significant to note that the predominant source of the tax gap is business income reported on 1040s, which is a much lower "visibility" income source that is not subject to the same information reporting and withholding requirements that exist for salary and wage income.

## IRS Actions to Improve Tax Compliance

Since 2001, IRS tax collections have increased significantly, audit rates have improved across all taxpayer segments, and the IRS has expanded its service options. But much work remains to be done, which is why the Administration has called for an increase in funding for the IRS for FY 2013.

The IRS has been and remains committed to improving voluntary compliance, which is the cornerstone of our tax system. The importance of voluntary compliance cannot be overstated: An additional percentage point of voluntary compliance brings in about $25 billion in tax receipts. Therefore, loss of public confidence in the proficiency and fairness of the IRS would come at a high cost, and the effects of a reduction in compliance would take a long time to reverse.

At the same time, the IRS recognizes that increased enforcement alone is not the answer. Put another way, we cannot simply audit our way out of the tax gap. The burden on taxpayers and on IRS resources would be too great. That is why the IRS continues to combine efforts against tax evasion with other measures, such as enhanced research techniques, improvements in information technology, and partnering with stakeholders such as states and foreign governments that also have a vested interest in increased taxpayer compliance.

Following is a description of some of our major initiatives:

- **Return preparers.** The IRS initiated a comprehensive review of the tax return preparation industry in 2009. A multifaceted return preparer strategy was launched in 2010 to ensure top-notch, professional and ethical service to taxpayers. Prior to this initiative, only CPAs, attorneys and Enrolled Agents were subject to professional credentialing, which together represented an estimated 39 percent of paid preparers. As a result of this compliance strategy, which is being phased in over several years; all paid return preparers will be registered with the IRS and identified on the returns they prepare. In addition, all paid preparers who are not CPAs, attorneys or Enrolled Agents will have to pass a competency exam and complete annual continuing education requirements related to tax law and professional conduct. This compliance strategy will cut down on inaccurate and fraudulent returns, help the IRS catch unscrupulous return preparers and improve service to taxpayers so that they are better able to comply with filing requirements.
- **Business taxes.** A major initiative in this area involves business tax audits. In recent years, the IRS has improved its focus in business audits more toward issues with the highest compliance risk. Risk-based audit selection leads to a more efficient use of limited resources

and a higher return on investment. The IRS continues to improve its exam selection procedures to focus on the most-pressing issues.

- **Employment taxes.** One of the major ongoing issues the IRS faces in the employment tax area involves companies that misclassify their workers as independent contractors instead of employees, and fail to withhold and remit employment tax on these workers. Last fall the IRS announced a new voluntary worker classification settlement program, which allows companies to voluntarily reclassify workers who have been misclassified. Participating companies get substantial relief from federal payroll taxes they may have owed if they prospectively treat workers as employees. Participants must make a minimal payment covering past payroll tax obligations, but they will not be charged interest or penalties.
- **Basis reporting.** As stated above, third-party reporting and transparency are crucial to a high voluntary compliance rate among individual taxpayers. Basis reporting associated with the buying and selling of securities was an area that was in need of third-party reporting based on previous studies that showed low levels of compliance. The IRS issued proposed regulations in 2009 and final regulations in 2010 under a new law that requires reporting of basis and other information by stockbrokers and mutual fund companies for most stock purchased in 2011 and all stock purchased in 2012 and later years. The reporting will be made to investors and to the IRS.
- **Credit card reporting.** Another major initiative in the area of third-party reporting and transparency involves new merchant card reporting requirements, which were established for the 2011 tax year. They provide third-party reporting data on business receipts for the first time, making it easier for the IRS to identify businesses that are either under-reporting receipts or not reporting at all. In general, these requirements apply to government entities and private businesses, as well as most types of payment cards, such as credit and debit cards. To help ease the transition to this new reporting system, the IRS provided penalty relief to filers for one year, through 2012.
- **Offshore tax avoidance.** Stopping offshore tax cheating and getting these taxpayers, especially high-net-worth individuals, back into the tax system has been a top priority of the IRS. A special offshore voluntary disclosure program was made available in 2009 and again in 2011, and these programs have encouraged more than 33,000 taxpayers to get right with the U.S. tax system while generating

billions of dollars in back taxes, interest and penalties. In January, we reopened the special offshore voluntary disclosure program, which will allow us to bring still more taxpayers with offshore accounts into compliance. Offshore tax avoidance is also being addressed through actions against foreign banks that have helped U.S. taxpayers hide their assets. A landmark enforcement victory against a Swiss bank in 2009 has led to the erosion of Swiss bank secrecy, and work by the IRS and the Justice Department continues in this area. There are other international efforts, including the creation of the Global High Wealth unit in November 2009, which was formed to better cope with the growing complexity of income and assets of the high-wealth population.

- **Uncertain tax positions.** In 2011, certain large corporations were required to start making so-called uncertain tax position (UTP) disclosures on their 2010 tax returns. The IRS issued the final UTP Schedule and instructions in September 2010. Reporting of uncertain tax positions fosters compliance by speeding up the time it takes to find issues and complete exams. It also helps the IRS work through corporate returns more efficiently and see where further guidance is needed to reduce uncertainty. An uncertain tax position is generally defined as a stance on a tax return where the corporation sets aside a reserve to either pay the higher amount of tax later or litigate the matter in the future.
- **Real time tax system.** The IRS has started exploring how to implement a series of long-term changes to the tax system which would result in higher levels of tax compliance. Under this concept of a "real time" tax system, the IRS would move away from the traditional "look-back" model of compliance, and instead perform substantially more upfront information return matching with tax returns when they are first filed with the IRS. The goal of this initiative is to improve the tax filing process by reducing burden for taxpayers and improving overall compliance.
- **Refund fraud.** Over the past few years the IRS has seen a significant increase in refund fraud schemes in general and schemes involving identity theft in particular. Overall, the IRS identified and prevented the issuance of more than $14 billion in fraudulent refunds in 2011. Our work in the area of refund fraud is a major endeavor and involves a multifaceted strategy. Our efforts to combat refund fraud related to

identity theft are a subset of this program, and further details of what we are doing in this area are outlined below.

- **Earned Income Tax Credit (EITC).** Reducing improper payments in the EITC program is a top priority for the IRS. We have taken a two-pronged approach to dealing with this problem. We perform outreach to help people understand the eligibility requirements before they file a claim. We also have a robust enforcement program that uses a variety of traditional and nontraditional methods. The EITC improper payment rate dropped from 26.3 percent in FY 2010 to 23.5 percent in FY 2011. This corresponds to a reduction in improper payments from $16.9 billion in FY 2010 to $15.2 billion in FY 2011.
- **Nonfilers and underreporters.** Over the last several years, the IRS has enhanced its technology capabilities, including software programs and document matching, to improve our ability to identify cases where taxpayers have failed to file a return or failed to report the correct amount of income. In FY 2011, the IRS closed 4.7 million document matching cases in our Automated Underreporter (AUR) program, up 47 percent from FY 2006. We also closed 1.4 million cases in our nonfiler program, known as Automated Substitute for Return (ASFR) in FY 2011, up 69 percent from FY 2006.
- **Assisting taxpayers.** Along with robust enforcement, a key component of the IRS efforts to shrink the tax gap involves easing burdens on taxpayers to make it easier for them to understand and to pay the taxes they owe. For example, under our Fresh Start initiative, in 2011 and again this year, we added new flexibilities to our collection program. Among other things, these flexibilities give more taxpayers the chance to set up installment agreements or apply for Offers in Compromise (OIC), which in turn allows the IRS to capture more in back taxes than we otherwise would have been able to collect.
- **Improvements in compliance research.** Keeping track of noncompliance in the presence of changing tax law and changing economic conditions, and conducting research on ways to increase compliance, are top priorities at the IRS. Research that is produced out of the NRP directly informs the models and algorithms that the IRS uses to target resources to the areas of highest compliance risk.

In: Tax Gaps
Editor: Rondell Meinke
ISBN: 978-1-62417-452-0


*Chapter 3*

# TESTIMONY OF J. RUSSELL GEORGE, TREASURY INSPECTOR GENERAL FOR TAX ADMINISTRATION. HEARING ON "PROBLEMS AT THE INTERNAL REVENUE SERVICE: CLOSING THE TAX GAP AND PREVENTING IDENTITY THEFT"*

Chairman Platts, Ranking Member Towns, and Members of the Subcommittee, I thank you for the opportunity to testify on the Tax Gap and the efforts by the Internal Revenue Service (IRS) to enforce compliance with the tax code.

My comments will focus on how the Treasury Inspector General for Tax Administration (TIGTA) provides oversight of the IRS's efforts to ensure that taxpayers comply with their tax obligations.

The IRS defines the Tax Gap as the difference between the estimated amount taxpayers owe[1] and the amount they voluntarily and timely pay for a tax year. In January 2012, the IRS released updated estimates of the Tax Gap for Tax Year (TY)[2] 2006, which indicated that the Nation's voluntary compliance rate was essentially unchanged from the prior estimates. The IRS states that the increase in the dollar amount is due almost entirely to the increase in total tax liabilities over the intervening period and does not reflect

* This is an edited, reformatted and augmented version of a Testimony Presented April 19, 2012 before the House Committee on Oversight and Government Reform, Subcommittee on Government Organization, Efficiency and Financial Management.

any significant change in compliance rates. The following table shows the comparison between the prior and the current Tax Gap estimates.

| | Tax Year 2001 (billions) | Tax Year 2006 (billions) |
|---|---|---|
| Total Tax Liabilities | $2,112 | $2,660 |
| Gross Tax Gap | $345 (83.7% compliance) | $450 (83.1% compliance) |
| Enforcement and Late Payments | $55 | $65 |
| Net Tax Gap | $290 | $385 |

The Gross Tax Gap is defined as the amount of true tax liability that taxpayers do not pay on time. The Net Tax Gap is defined as the amount of true tax liability that is not paid on time and is not collected subsequently, either voluntarily or as the result of enforcement activities.

The IRS reports that the Gross Tax Gap is comprised of three primary components:

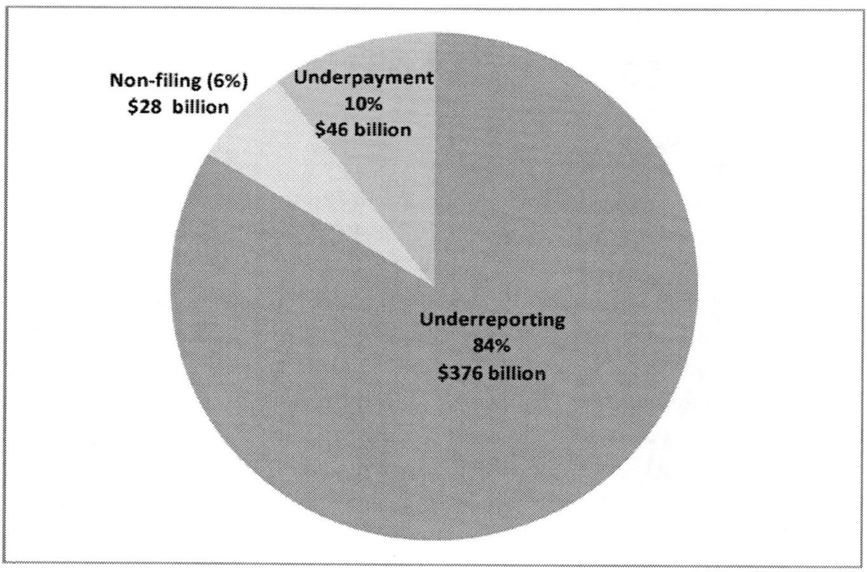


- Underreporting of tax liabilities. Of the $450 billion gross Tax Gap in TY 2006, $376 billion (approximately 84 percent) is estimated to result from the underreporting of tax liabilities. Specifically, the underreporting Tax Gap (henceforth the “underreporting gap”) is defined as the amount of tax liability not voluntarily reported by taxpayers who file required returns on time. For income taxes, the underreporting gap arises from three types of errors: underreporting taxable income, overstating offsets to income or to tax, and net math errors. Taxable income includes such items as wages and salaries, rents and royalties, and net business income. Offsets to income include income exclusions, exemptions, statutory adjustments, and deductions. Offsets to tax are tax credits. Net math errors involve mathematical mistakes or transcription errors made by taxpayers that are corrected at the time the return is processed. In addition to developing an estimate of the aggregate underreporting gap, it is possible to break aspects of this estimate down into measures of the underreporting gap attributable to specific line items on the tax return.

- Non-filing of tax returns. Of the $450 billion gross Tax Gap in TY 2006, $28 billion (approximately 6 percent) is estimated to be associated with tax returns that were filed after the filing deadline (or valid extension date) or were not filed at all. It is reduced by amounts paid on time, such as through withholding, estimated payments, and other credits. However, it does not include legitimate nonfilers (i.e., those who have no obligation to file).
- Underpayment of tax liabilities. For TY 2006, $46 billion of taxes reported on time were not paid when due. Stated another way, the underpayment gap is the portion of the total tax liability that taxpayers report on their timely filed returns but do not pay on time. This arises primarily from insufficient remittances from taxpayers themselves. However, it also includes employer under-deposits of withheld income tax. In the case of withheld income tax, employees have the responsibility to report the corresponding tax liability on timely filed returns, and employers are responsible for depositing those withholdings with the Government on time.

The IRS reported that the growth in the Tax Gap from TY 2001 to 2006 was concentrated in the underreporting and underpayment forms of noncompliance, which jointly account for more than nine out of ten Tax Gap dollars. The underreporting gap grew by 32 percent and the underpayment gap grew by 38 percent. In contrast, the nonfiling gap grew by only 4 percent.

The IRS further reported that more than a third of the growth in the underreporting gap was attributable to corporate income taxes. Several factors contributed to this increase: First, the 2001 estimate was calculated based on old data and was likely understated. Second, the new estimate relied on more recent and improved data. And finally, between TY 2001 and 2006, corporate income tax liabilities more than doubled, while the individual income taxes grew by only 15 percent.

Compliance is far higher when reported amounts on tax returns are subject to information reporting and withholding. For example, when there is substantial information reporting and withholding[3] the compliance rate is 99 percent. For amounts subject to substantial information reporting but not withholding,[4] the rate is 92 percent. For amounts subject to little or no information reporting, such as business income, the rate is only 44 percent.

The IRS reported that for TY 2006, the amount of enforced and other late payments it will eventually collect is estimated to be $65 billion. Both types of payments were estimated using IRS data of prior revenue and late payments received. However, the IRS does not have good data on the amounts that are paid late without enforcement efforts, and amounts to be collected in future years were estimated using data on payment patterns from earlier years.

The IRS uses a variety of techniques to identify unpaid tax liabilities, including (1) identifying taxpayers who file tax returns without fully paying the tax reported to be owed, (2) checking for obvious errors when processing returns, (3) finding additional tax liabilities by auditing a filed tax return, (4) assessing a penalty for some taxpayer action or inaction, and (5) sending a bill to a taxpayer who did not file a required tax return.

If the taxpayer does not cooperate, the IRS may take enforced collection action. Enforcement action could include serving a notice of levy that is attached to the taxpayer's income or assets such as bank accounts. In some cases, the IRS will take enforcement action by seizing and selling property. The IRS takes these actions only after giving the taxpayer an opportunity to voluntarily pay the debt, make arrangements to pay, or supply information to show that payment would create a hardship.

In the IRS's 2007 report on *Reducing the Federal Tax Gap*, the IRS states that voluntary compliance rates appear to have remained relatively stable at around 85 percent for decades. The report further states that to make a meaningful improvement in this rate will require a long-term, focused effort involving taxpayer service, modernization, and enforcement. The Department of the Treasury's 2006 report, *A Comprehensive Strategy for Reducing the Tax Gap,* describes the extensive challenges to reducing the Tax Gap. According to the report, addressing the Tax Gap involves improving voluntary compliance, reducing opportunities for evasion through legislative proposals, and making it easier for the IRS to administer the tax laws, accompanied by broader simplification and reform of the tax code and significant advances in compliance technology.

The IRS also reported that the Tax Gap is caused by both unintentional taxpayer errors (whether due to tax law complexity, confusion, ignorance, or carelessness) and willful tax evasion or cheating, although the IRS does not have sufficient data to distinguish the amounts attributable to each. In addition, a wide range of factors influence voluntary compliance, including tax law changes, the economy, and changing demographics of the taxpayer population. There are also indirect effects of IRS enforcement activities beyond the direct effects of additional revenue collections. These refer to "spillover" effects when enforcement activity on one set of taxpayers has positive effects on the compliance behavior of the rest of the taxpayer population in response to heightened enforcement activity. However, the IRS also stated that it is very difficult to determine the impact that any IRS activity has on voluntary compliance.

From the perspective of tax administration, the IRS also needs to overcome institutional impediments to more effectively address the Tax Gap. These impediments refer to the established policies, practices, technologies, business processes or requirements that add unintended costs or are no longer optimal given changes to strategies, goals, and technologies. TIGTA's perspective is that the current institutional impediments the IRS faces can point the way to improvement opportunities, to wit:

- *Incomplete compliance research* that does not identify all the sources of noncompliance so that IRS resources can be targeted properly. The IRS reported that new research is needed on the relationship between taxpayer burden and compliance and on the impact of customer service on voluntary compliance. Additional research would also assist in establishing benchmarks and measures to assess the effectiveness of IRS efforts to address taxpayer compliance.
- *Insufficient compliance strategies* that do not always address the areas of highest risk of noncompliance. The IRS's systems that identify returns for examination need improvement. IRS examinations continue to result in no change to the return, resulting in an inefficient use of examination resources and increased burden on compliant taxpayers. In addition, IRS collection activity that extends for years has a lower rate of collection for delinquent liabilities. The IRS reported it is working to reengineer examination and collection procedures based on improved data from its National Research Project

study of individual taxpayers. This effort, coupled with investments in technology, should result in efficiency gains and better targeting of examination efforts. These efficiency gains translate into expanded examination coverage, higher audit yields, and reduced burden on compliant taxpayers.

- *Incomplete document matching programs* because the IRS does not have reliable third-party data for all taxpayer sectors and for all types of tax returns, most notably income earned by the self-employed. The IRS reported that, without this data, it cannot easily detect errors or potential fraud except through expensive and intrusive examinations.
- *Insufficient enforcement resources* to handle a growing caseload. The IRS has identified noncompliance and potential fraud cases it did not have the resources to work, allowing billions of dollars to be fraudulently refunded each year.[5] In addition, in Fiscal Year[6] (FY) 2010, the Collection function was unable to work all of the existing accounts in the Queue[7] with current staffing, and the number of new taxpayer delinquent accounts was outpacing closures. If changes do not occur, a significant number of cases will continue to not receive additional contact to resolve the tax delinquency.[8]

The IRS often faces constant changes as a result of temporary tax provisions and new tax law. For example, during FY 2010, the IRS encountered many challenges, including a variety of tax provisions that were created, extended, or expanded. Specifically, the provisions were the:

- *American Recovery and Reinvestment Act of 2009 (Recovery Act).*[9] The Recovery Act included 56 tax provisions (20 related to individual taxpayers and 36 related to business taxpayers). These provisions will continue to challenge the IRS over multiple filing seasons.
- *Worker, Homeownership, and Business Assistance Act of 2009.*[10] The Worker, Homeownership, and Business Assistance Act of 2009 revised, extended, and expanded the First-Time Homebuyer Credit (Homebuyer Credit) to a broader range of home purchases and added new documentation requirements. Initially, the IRS did not have math error authority[11] to disallow the Homebuyer Credit during processing if documentation was not provided. Congress has since passed legislation requiring documentation for the Homebuyer Credit and provided the IRS with math error authority to disallow the Credit if the documentation was not provided.

- *Hiring Incentives to Restore Employment Act of 2010 (HIRE Act).*[12] The HIRE Act enacted tax benefits to employers who expanded payrolls and hired previously unemployed individuals. Eligible business taxpayers will be exempt from their share of Social Security taxes on wages to eligible employees. These taxpayers may also be eligible for a credit of up to $1,000 for qualified employees. Additionally, Title V of the HIRE Act included the Foreign Account Tax Compliance Act. A provision of this Act included the requirement that individual taxpayers indicate on their income tax returns the maximum value of foreign financial assets held during the tax year. This provision will allow the IRS to increase enforcement on taxpayers hiding assets overseas.
- *Patient Protection and Affordable Care Act of 2010 (Affordable Care Act).*[13] At least 42 of the 514 Affordable Care Act provisions add to or amend the Internal Revenue Code, and at least eight require the IRS to establish new operations. Collectively, these provisions represent the largest set of tax law changes in 20 years. The Affordable Care Act contains $438 billion of revenue provisions in the form of new taxes and fees. It also contains credits which provide incentives for medical research and for businesses to offer employees health care insurance. Additionally, new reporting requirements have been established for certain business transactions. The Affordable Care Act further imposes penalties administered through the tax code for individuals and businesses that do not obtain health coverage for themselves or their employees. Other provisions raise revenue to help pay for the overall cost of health insurance reform.

These tax provisions are examples of the impact that tax law changes have on how the IRS conducts its activities, how many resources are required, and how quickly or whether the IRS can meet strategic goals. The IRS has the challenging task of maintaining a quality workforce and enforcing tax laws in an environment of constantly changing tax legislation.

The IRS also faces significant challenges in obtaining complete and timely compliance data and in developing methods necessary to interpret the data. Despite a 19 percent increase in enforcement staffing levels since FY 2006 and the IRS's more vigorous use of collection enforcement tools, FY 2010 enforcement results were mixed when compared to FY 2009 results. The number of delinquent accounts closed by full payment and the amount collected on delinquent accounts increased. However, the Collection function received more delinquent accounts than it closed, gross accounts receivable rose, and the number of tax delinquency investigation cases[14] closed with the receipt of a delinquent tax return fell.[15] In addition, there were increases in the number of delinquent accounts that may never be worked because they were shelved or surveyed and in accounts receivable. For examinations, the large staffing level increases in FY 2009 and FY 2010 resulted in the most tax returns examined in the past five years. The dollar yield per hour for examinations increased in FY 2009 but decreased in FY 2010. In addition, the no-change rates[16] for several types of examinations increased in FY 2010 compared to FY 2009. The IRS continues to conduct studies with the goal of improving the return selection process to increase rates of return across the enforcement program.

One means the IRS employs to collect unpaid taxes is the notice stream.[17] The notice stream is the least costly of the IRS's approaches to collecting unpaid taxes. While the notice stream collects billions of dollars in delinquent taxes annually, reducing the time between notices could result in the annual collection of millions of dollars more. During FY 2010, the IRS sent approximately 21.9 million balance-due notices to individuals to attempt to collect unpaid taxes.

By a wide margin, the first notice (also known as the Master File notice) closed the most cases, collected the most money, and generated the highest number of taxpayer responses. Cases not resolved after the Master File notice continue in the notice stream, and those taxpayers receive various sequences of notices.

The IRS allows 35 days between notices for the taxpayer to respond, but TIGTA's analysis shows that the time between notices can be reduced. As these balance due modules progress within the notice stream, the probability of collection diminishes.

TIGTA recommended that the IRS consider reducing the time between each notice by seven days. This could result in the potential collection of as much as $363 million more each year. In addition, taxpayers could potentially save $1.8 million each year in interest payments. The IRS agreed with TIGTA's recommendations and plans to take corrective actions. However, in its response, the IRS stated that 35 days between notices were necessary to process taxpayer inquiries and correspondence. TIGTA's report noted that the IRS has controls in place to prevent the next notice from being sent when taxpayers' correspondence is being processed.[18]

The IRS reported the following initiatives that it has begun to implement to address the Tax Gap.

## TAX RETURN PREPARERS

Every year, more than one-half of all taxpayers pay someone else to prepare their Federal income tax returns. During the 2011 Filing Season,[19] the IRS processed approximately 66.9 million individual Federal income tax returns prepared by paid tax return preparers.

In December 2009, the IRS announced a suite of proposed reforms to improve oversight of the return preparer community. TIGTA is monitoring the IRS's implementation of the new Return Preparer Program. In September 2011, TIGTA reported that it will take years for the IRS to implement the Return Preparer Program and to realize its impact.[20] When the decision was made to register preparers, the IRS had not established all of the program requirements. The IRS also had not: (1) established the organizational structure of the program, (2) determined how it will verify that all preparers met the requirements, (3) determined how it will enforce program requirements, or (4) developed the system(s) and processes necessary to administer and oversee the program. It will not be until Calendar Year[21] 2014 that all preparers will be subjected to all suitability and competency tests. In the meantime, IRS management stated they will develop and implement an enforcement strategy. Currently, the IRS does not have a sufficient management information system to gather data on preparers. Further, the IRS will need to ensure that taxpayers understand the new requirements and the importance of using only registered preparers to prepare their tax returns.

Of the 66.9 million individual Federal income tax returns prepared by paid tax return preparers and processed by the IRS in Calendar Year 2011, 90 percent were e-filed.[22] In November 2009, Congress approved a Federal e-file mandate for tax return preparers. TIGTA's review of the IRS's implementation of the mandate found that for the first few years, the IRS plans to use a "soft" approach to enforcement that emphasizes educating and collaborating with preparers in implementing e-file requirements. Additionally, the continued use of multiple preparer identification numbers makes it difficult to match all tax returns to the preparers. However, improvements are under way to ensure the effectiveness of controls and system validations over the preparer registration process.

TIGTA recommended several actions, including that the IRS monitor preparers' compliance with the e-file mandate and ensure that suitability tests match applicants to IRS information to identify preparers who are not allowed to prepare tax returns. IRS management agreed and stated that corrective actions to address the recommendations have been taken or are planned.

The IRS reported that this compliance strategy will cut down on inaccurate and fraudulent returns. It also makes it easier for the IRS to catch unscrupulous return preparers. In addition, these efforts will help improve service to taxpayers and assist with voluntary compliance.

## Basis Reporting

Third-party reporting and transparency is also crucial to high compliance among individual taxpayers. Basis reporting associated with the buying and selling of securities was an area that needed third-party reporting based on previous studies that showed low levels of compliance.

The IRS issued proposed regulations in 2009 and final regulations in 2010 under a new law[23] that will require reporting by stock brokers and mutual fund companies on an investor's adjusted basis and whether any gain or loss on the sale is classified as short-term or long-term for most stock purchased in 2011 and all stock purchased in 2012 and later years. Such reports will be made available to investors and the IRS.

## Business Taxes

Third-party reporting and transparency are hallmarks of high levels of tax compliance. The IRS undertook several initiatives in recent years to improve those aspects in the world of business taxes, where the efficient allocation of limited resources is particularly important to sound tax administration.

New merchant card reporting requirements[24] were established for TY 2011. They provide third-party reporting data on business receipts for the first time, making it easier for the IRS to identify businesses that are either under-reporting receipts or not reporting at all. The IRS issued final regulations in 2010 and the new reporting requirements took effect on January 1, 2011. In general, these requirements apply to government entities and private businesses, as well as most types of payment cards, such as credit and debit cards.

In an effort to achieve greater transparency, the IRS also requires the reporting of certain tax avoidance transactions that have the potential to be abusive. These transactions are called "listed" transactions and also include other types of transactions that are the same or substantially similar to the listed transactions. Taxpayers are required to disclose their participation in listed transactions or they may be subject to penalties. In FY 2010, the IRS received approximately 35,000 of the disclosure documents.

## INTERNATIONAL COMPLIANCE EFFORTS

Globalization of the U.S. economy has been a major trend for many years. International business holdings and investment in the United States have grown from nearly $188 billion in 1976 to over $14.5 trillion in 2007, while U.S. business and investment worldwide grew from nearly $368 billion to nearly $15 trillion over the same period. The scope and complexity of the international financial system create significant enforcement challenges for the IRS. The IRS continues to be challenged by a lack of information reporting on many cross-border transactions. In addition, the varying legal requirements imposed by different jurisdictions result in complex business structures that make it difficult to determine the full scope and effect of these cross-border transactions. Technological advances also provide opportunities for offshore investments that were once only possible for large corporations and wealthy individuals.

Over the past few years, the IRS has taken steps and made strategic internal realignments to better coordinate international tax compliance issues. It has developed a strategic plan specifically for international tax issues with two major goals: 1) enforce the law to ensure that all taxpayers meet their obligation to pay U.S. taxes and 2) improve service to make voluntary compliance less burdensome. In November 2009, the IRS's Global High Wealth unit began operation. It was formed to better cope with the growing complexity of income and assets of the high-income, high-wealth population. In August 2010, the IRS realigned its international efforts under its Large Business and International (LB&I) Division, which was designed to strengthen international tax enforcement in several ways, including identifying emerging international compliance issues more quickly and ensuring the right compliance resources are allocated to the right cases. During FY 2012, the IRS will merge the Office of Chief Counsel's Advanced Pricing Agreement Program with the LB&I Division's Mutual Agreement Program to form the Advanced Pricing and Mutual Agreement Program. This combined program will be a component of the LB&I Division's Transfer Pricing Operations. The IRS expects that efforts like these will improve international tax compliance by allowing it to focus on high-risk issues and cases with greater consistency and efficiency.

The Congress, the Department of the Treasury, and the IRS are concerned about the International Tax Gap – that is, taxes owed, but not collected on time, from a U.S. or nonresident person whose cross-border income is subject to U.S. taxation. The IRS has not estimated the size of the International Tax Gap, but non-IRS estimates range from $40 billion to $123 billion[25] annually. While there might be overlap between the overall IRS Tax Gap estimate and the International Tax Gap estimate, it is unlikely that the $450 billion Tax Gap estimate includes the entire International Tax Gap. The primary reason for this is that identifying hidden income within international activity is very difficult and time-consuming.[26]

The IRS's strategic initiatives focus on strengthening reporting requirements, enhancing IRS access to international data, and aligning resources to cases and issues with the highest compliance risk. One reporting requirement is the *Report of Foreign Bank and Financial Accounts* (FBAR) report, which is an information report required when U.S. citizens, residents, and domestic entities owns or has signature or other authority over foreign financial accounts worth over $10,000 in any calendar year. Congress set up FBAR penalties because some taxpayers use these foreign accounts to evade U.S. taxation.

In addition, the Foreign Account Tax Compliance Act (FATCA) [27] requires foreign financial institutions to report to the IRS information about financial accounts held by U.S. taxpayers or by foreign entities in which U.S. taxpayers hold a substantial ownership interest. FATCA will be phased in by the IRS in the next several years. Individual taxpayers with an aggregate balance of more than $50,000 in foreign financial assets are required to file a disclosure statement with their income tax return.

In August 2010, TIGTA reported that taxpayers excluded $19.2 billion in foreign earned income on TY 2008 tax returns. Our review identified 23,334 tax returns with erroneous foreign earned income tax exclusions totaling $675 million, with an estimated revenue loss of $90 million. Over five years, TIGTA estimated erroneous claims could result in a total revenue loss of $450 million. Some of the recommendations that TIGTA provided were that the IRS:

- Review the tax returns of those individuals that TIGTA identified as incorrectly claiming the foreign earned income exclusion;

- Establish a unit to address taxpayers identified as erroneously claiming the foreign earned income exclusion;
- Assess whether compliance project criteria can be used to identify erroneous claims during tax return processing; and
- Include programming to forward tax returns (both electronically filed and paper) for correction when individuals incorrectly compute their foreign earned income exclusion.

IRS management agreed with most of the recommendations, but they stated that substantial barriers prevented the implementation of certain recommendations at the time of the review. TIGTA is concerned that the lack of corrective actions will allow continued revenue loss.[28]

## OFFSHORE TAX AVOIDANCE

Stopping offshore tax cheating and getting these people, especially high net-worth individuals, back into the tax system has been a top priority of the IRS. The IRS continues to work with the U.S. Department of Justice on tax evasion cases involving foreign countries with bank secrecy laws that prevent the United States from obtaining information on taxpayer transactions. In addition, both the 2009 and 2011 Offshore Voluntary Disclosure Initiatives have encouraged taxpayers with hidden offshore assets and income to come back into the tax system using the IRS's Voluntary Disclosure Program. According to the IRS, these initiatives have resulted in the collection of over $4 billion. Due to the success of the first two initiatives, the IRS is currently offering a third chance for delinquent taxpayers to disclose their hidden offshore assets. These initiatives are beneficial because they offer a uniform penalty structure for taxpayers who voluntarily disclose their hidden offshore assets and income to the IRS and, in return, ensure that the taxpayers receive consistent tax and penalty treatment.

The initiatives also provide the opportunity to calculate, with a reasonable degree of certainty, the total cost of resolving all outstanding offshore tax issues related to the undisclosed foreign bank and financial accounts and assets. On the other hand, taxpayers with undisclosed foreign accounts and assets who do not submit a voluntary disclosure run the risk of detection by the IRS. If caught, these taxpayers face the imposition of substantial penalties, including the fraud and foreign information return penalties, as well as an increased risk of criminal prosecution.

## REAL-TIME TAX SYSTEM

The IRS has started work exploring how to implement a series of long-term changes to the tax system which will result in higher compliance. Commissioner Shulman has described a vision where the IRS would move away from the traditional "look-back" model of compliance, and instead endeavor to conduct its compliance efforts in "real time," such as by matching third-party information with information provided by the taxpayer when the tax returns are first filed with the IRS.

The goal of this initiative is to improve the tax filing process by reducing burden for taxpayers and improving overall compliance "up front," during the filing season instead of later through compliance or enforcement activities. In addition, the IRS plans to include more data mining and predictive analytics in this initiative, to improve identification of noncompliance and potential tax fraud.

In FY 2012, the IRS has delivered significant updates to its core tax processing system, transitioning to a daily processing cycle for individual returns. Also, IRS processing systems are accepting all Forms 1040, U.S. Individual Income Tax Return, electronically through an updated e-filing capability. This capability is designed to eventually feed into a single, consolidated taxpayer account database that will support the deployment of the next generation of taxpayer service and enforcement functions.

TIGTA has reviewed a number of other IRS challenges in addressing the Tax Gap. One important aspect involves human capital. Like many Federal agencies, the IRS is faced with the major challenge of replacing existing talent caused by a large number of retirements expected over the next several years. In five years, about one-third of the IRS's workforce of approximately 100,000 employees will be retirement eligible. This statistic is even more pronounced in the leadership ranks, where over two-thirds of IRS executives will be retirement eligible in five years. Adding to this challenge, the IRS offered early retirement and buyouts to more than 2,200 employees in FY 2011.

Replacing these employees provides an opportunity for reshaping the IRS workforce, but also represents a significant challenge since many departing employees possess unique skills and institutional knowledge that will be difficult to replace.

Revenue officers (RO) have a direct impact on the IRS's ability to meet its mission by collecting the appropriate amount of tax due. The IRS added 1,515 new ROs during the period June 2009 through February 2010, but it still struggles to keep pace with attrition and workload. If the IRS does not have a sufficient number of qualified ROs to collect delinquent taxes, it could create an unfair burden on the majority of taxpayers who fully pay their taxes on time. However, when estimating the staffing levels of ROs, the IRS does not determine the number needed to address the available workload. Instead, the IRS bases the RO staffing level primarily on a budget figure. The IRS believes there is more than enough inventory to justify staffing increases. However, the IRS does not know when hiring additional ROs will no longer be needed.

The IRS's FY 2009 budget justification projected that the RO hiring initiative would allow 88,000 additional delinquent account closures, resulting in $333.6 million in additional revenue for FY 2011. However, the IRS does not track a comparison of actual results to the original projections in the years following the budget's implementation. As a result, it is unknown if the IRS realized all or part of the additional projected revenue for this initiative, and the IRS lost an opportunity to collect information that could help improve future budgets. TIGTA recommended that the IRS:

- Establish rules for optimizing staffing levels for ROs to address Collection's potentially collectible inventory; and
- Develop methods to track actual results with projected benefits in future budget justifications.

IRS management agreed to review workload and resource levels to improve future resource allocation and staffing decisions. IRS management also stated that they initiated efforts in 2010 to develop a methodology to determine the actual revenue collected from specific enforcement initiatives proposed in the IRS's FY 2009 budget justification.

However, this information was not shared with TIGTA during the review. As a result, TIGTA did not assess whether those efforts addressed the recommendation.[29] Until IRS management implements this type of methodology, they will not know the actual additional revenue realized from requested enforcement initiatives.

The misclassification of millions of employees as independent contractors is a nationwide problem that continues to grow and contribute to the $72 billion underreporting Employment Tax Gap. In a report issued in Fiscal Year 2010,[30] TIGTA determined that the IRS has opportunities to enhance compliance in its Employment Tax Program by: 1) taking measures to ensure employment tax forms are not misused to avoid paying taxes, and 2) regularly sharing the results of worker classification examinations between IRS compliance functions to ensure the greatest possible use of the agency's resources when addressing the underreporting Tax Gap. TIGTA identified more than 74,000 taxpayers who may have avoided paying approximately $26 million in Social Security and Medicare taxes in Processing Year[31] 2008.

Another of the IRS's priorities is combating tax avoidance transactions.[32] However, the IRS has identified tax returns with tax avoidance transaction issues that do not warrant examination before taxpayer contact, a process known as surveying.

Surveying tax returns with a tax avoidance transaction issue without proper justification or approval could be counterproductive to the IRS's goal to combat abusive schemes.

In addition, this approach can erode the public's confidence in the IRS's ability to enforce tax laws in a fair, equitable, and consistent manner. As a result, TIGTA recommended that the IRS:

- Develop internal controls and train employees to ensure that justification is in the case files to survey tax returns with a tax avoidance transaction issue;
- Have an independent function review the tax return for concurrence with the group manager's decision;
- Ensure that tax returns with tax avoidance transaction issues (surveyed as excess inventory) can be readily identified, and examinations are completed once taxpayers are contacted; and
- Develop procedures to ensure surveyed tax returns are included as part of the quality review process.

IRS management disagreed with TIGTA's two recommendations related to strengthening existing controls and developing procedures to include surveyed tax returns as part of the quality review process. TIGTA continues to believe that the breakdown in controls for the approval process indicates that tax returns surveyed without documentation may have yielded examination results.

## QUALITY TAXPAYER SERVICE

The Department of the Treasury and the IRS recognize that the delivery of effective taxpayer service has a significant impact on voluntary tax compliance. Answering taxpayers' questions to assist them to correctly prepare their returns reduces the need to send notices and correspondence when taxpayers make errors. Taxpayer service also reduces unintentional noncompliance and shrinks the need for future collection activity. The IRS continues to focus on the importance of improving service by emphasizing it as a main goal in its strategic plan. It is also seeking innovative ways to simplify or eliminate processes that unnecessarily burden taxpayers or Government resources.

## End Notes

[1] This includes all types of tax liabilities, including: Individual Income Tax, Corporation Income Tax, Employment Tax, Estate Tax, and Excise Tax.

[2] A 12-month accounting period for keeping records on income and expenses used as the basis for calculating the annual taxes due. For most individual taxpayers, the tax year is synonymous with the calendar year.

[3] Wages and salaries.

[4] Pensions and annuities, unemployment compensation, dividend and interest income, Social Security benefits.

[5] TIGTA, Ref. No. 2011-40-023, Reduction Targets and Strategies Have Not Been Established to Reduce the Billions of Dollars in Improper Earned Income Tax Credit Payments Each Year (February 2011).

[6] A 12-consecutive-month period ending on the last day of any month, except December. The Federal Government's fiscal year begins on October 1 and ends on September 30.

[7] An automated holding file for unassigned inventory of delinquent cases for which the Collection function does not have enough resources to immediately assign the cases for contact.

[8] TIGTA, Ref. No. 2011-30-071, Trends in Compliance Activities Through Fiscal Year 2010 (July 2011).

[9] Pub. L. No. 111-5, 123 Stat. 115.

[10] Pub. L. No. 111-92, 123 Stat. 2984.

[11] This is a program in which the IRS contacts taxpayers through the mail or by telephone when it identifies mathematical errors or mismatches of taxpayer information that would result in a tax change.

[12] Pub. L. No. 111-147, 124 Stat. 71.

[13] Pub. L. No. 111-148, 124 Stat. 119.

[14] An unfiled tax return for a taxpayer. One tax delinquency investigation case exists for all tax periods.

[15] TIGTA, Ref. No. 2011-30-071, Trends in Compliance Activities Through Fiscal Year 2010 (July 2011).

[16] Percentage of examinations where the examiner closed the case with no recommended tax change.

[17] A series of balance-due notices sent by the IRS to the taxpayer to prompt payment.

[18] TIGTA, Ref. No. 2011-30-112, Reducing the Processing Time Between Balance Due Notices Could Increase Collections (September 2011).

[19] The period from January 1 through April 15 when most individual income tax returns are filed.

[20] TIGTA, Ref. No. 2010-40-127, It Will Take Years to Implement the Return Preparer Program and to Realize Its Impact (September 2010).

[21] The 12-consecutive-month period ending on December 31.

[22] As of May 4, 2011.

[23] Energy Improvement and Extension Act of 2008, Pub. L. No. 110-343, § 403, 122 Stat. 3765, 3854- 3858.

[24] Housing and Economic Recovery Act of 2008, sec. 3091, § 6050W, 112 Stat. 2654, 2908-2911.

[25] TIGTA, Ref. No. 2009-IE-R001, A Combination of Legislative Actions and Increased IRS Capability and Capacity Are Required to Reduce the Multi-Billion Dollar U.S. International Tax Gap (January 2009).

[26] GAO, Ref. No. GAO-07-237, Tax Administration: Additional Time Needed to Complete Offshore Tax Evasion Examinations (March 2007).

[27] In 2010, FATCA was enacted as part of the Hiring Incentives to Restore Employment (HIRE) Act, Pub. L. No. 111-147, 124 Stat. 71, 97-117.

[28] TIGTA, Ref. No. 2010-40-091, Improvements Are Needed to Reduce Erroneous Foreign Earned Income Exclusion Claims (August 2010).

[29] TIGTA, Ref. No. 2011-30-039, Challenges Remain to Balance Revenue Officer Staffing With Attrition and Workload Demands (May 2011).

[30] TIGTA, Ref. No. 2010-30-025, Employment Tax Compliance Could Be Improved With Better Coordination and Information Sharing (March 2010).

[31] The calendar year in which the tax return or document is processed by the IRS.

[32] A tax avoidance transaction is generally a specific tax transaction or promotion that reduces tax liability by taking a tax position that is not supported by tax law. These strategies may be organized and marketed, often through the Internet. The definition is not merely limited to activities that improperly reduce tax, but may also include transactions that conceal assets and income.

In: Tax Gaps
Editor: Rondell Meinke
ISBN: 978-1-62417-452-0


*Chapter 4*

# TAX GAP: SOURCES OF NONCOMPLIANCE AND STRATEGIES TO REDUCE IT. STATEMENT OF JAMES R. WHITE, DIRECTOR, STRATEGIC ISSUES, GOVERNMENT ACCOUNTABILITY OFFICE. HEARING ON "PROBLEMS AT THE INTERNAL REVENUE SERVICE: CLOSING THE TAX GAP AND PREVENTING IDENTITY THEFT"*

***United States Government Accountability Office***

## WHY GAO DID THIS STUDY

In January 2012, IRS estimated that the gross tax gap—the difference between taxes owed and taxes paid on time—was $450 billion for tax year 2006.

IRS estimated that it would collect $65 billion through enforcement actions and late payments, leaving a net tax gap of $385 billion. From 2001 to 2006, IRS estimated that the gross tax gap increased by $105 billion.

* This is an edited, reformatted and augmented version of The United States Government Accountability Office publication GAO-12-651T, dated April 19, 2012.

However, the percentage of taxes owed that were paid on time remained relatively constant at 83.1 percent in 2006, compared to 83.7 percent in 2001.

Given persistent levels of noncompliance and large and growing structural deficits, it will be important to understand the causes of tax noncompliance and develop new approaches to minimize it.

This testimony addresses two questions: (1) What types of taxpayers are responsible for the tax gap, and what is the nature of their noncompliance? (2) What are strategies for reducing the tax gap? The statement also discusses potential long-term strategies to prevent refund fraud related to identity theft. This statement is based largely on GAO's recent reports and recommendations on tax noncompliance and updates GAO's 2011 testimony on the tax gap.

## What GAO Recommends

GAO has made numerous prior recommendations regarding actions to close the tax gap. Congress and IRS have acted on some, while others are reflected in the strategies presented in this testimony.

## What GAO Found

Noncompliance does not have a single source but occurs across different types of taxes and taxpayers. For example, individual income tax accounts for the largest portion of the tax gap, but corporate income tax and employment tax are also significant. Further, misreporting by individuals involves business income, non-business income, deductions, and credits.

The extent of misreporting depends on the extent to which income tax is withheld or reported to the Internal Revenue Service (IRS) by third parties. For example, nearly 40 percent, or $179 billion, of the 2006 gross tax gap is due to misreporting of non-corporate business income and related self-employment taxes. Much of this misreporting can be attributed to sole proprietors underreporting receipts or over-reporting expenses. Unlike wage and some investment income, sole proprietors' income is not subject to withholding and only a portion is reported to IRS by third parties.Because noncompliance has multiple causes and spans different types of taxes and taxpayers, multiple approaches are needed to reduce the tax gap. The following strategies could help and will require actions by Congress or IRS.

*Enhancing information reporting by third parties to IRS* could reduce tax evasion and help taxpayers comply voluntarily. However, identifying additional reporting opportunities can be challenging because third parties may not have accurate information available in a timely manner. Also, adding reporting requirements creates burden for both third parties and IRS.

*Ensuring high-quality services to taxpayers*, such as by telephone and correspondence or online, can help taxpayers who wish to comply with tax laws but do not understand their obligations. However, tax law changes and funding priorities have recently affected IRS's ability to provide quality taxpayer services.

*Devoting additional resources to enforcement* would enable IRS to contact millions of potentially noncompliant taxpayers it identifies but cannot contact. To determine the appropriate level of enforcement resources, policymakers would need to consider how to balance taxpayer service and enforcement activities and how effectively and efficiently IRS currently uses its resources.

*Expanding compliance checks before IRS issues refunds* would involve matching information returns to tax returns during, rather than after, the tax filing season. This approach would require a major reworking of some fundamental IRS computer systems but could help address identity theft-related fraud and allow IRS to use enforcement resources on other compliance problems.

*Leveraging external resources, such as paid tax return preparers and whistleblowers,* can help improve tax compliance because paid preparers' actions have an enormous impact on IRS's ability to effectively administer tax laws, and whistleblowers provide IRS information on suspected noncompliance.

*Modernizing information systems* would allow IRS to post more comprehensive tax return information to its computer systems, which could facilitate the examination process and expedite taxpayer contacts for faster resolution.

*Simplifying the tax code* could help taxpayers understand and voluntarily comply with their tax obligations and limit opportunities for tax evasion.

Chairman Platts, Ranking Member Towns, and Members of the Subcommittee:

I am pleased to be here to discuss the tax gap and related fraud, such as identity theft based refund fraud, and how to reduce it. In January 2012, the

Internal Revenue Service (IRS) estimated that the gross tax gap—the difference between taxes owed and taxes paid on time—was $450 billion in tax year 2006. IRS estimated that it would eventually recover about $65 billion of this amount through late payments and enforcement actions, leaving a net tax gap of $385 billion.[1] The tax gap has been a persistent problem in spite of a myriad of congressional and IRS efforts to reduce it, as the rate at which taxpayers voluntarily comply with United States tax laws has changed little over the past three decades. In past testimonies, we have said that there are no easy fixes to this problem, and given persistent levels of noncompliance, reducing the tax gap will not likely be achieved through a single solution. Rather, the tax gap must be attacked on multiple fronts and with multiple strategies over a sustained period of time. Whether mistakes are intentional or unintentional, misreporting is unfair to compliant taxpayers and undermines the equity of the tax system. Moreover, in the face of large and growing structural deficits, it will be especially important to understand the causes of tax noncompliance today and continue to develop new approaches to minimize it.

My testimony today will answer two questions: (1) What types of taxpayers are responsible for the tax gap, and what is the nature of their noncompliance? (2) What are strategies for reducing the tax gap? As requested, we will also provide information on potential long-term strategies to prevent refund fraud related to identity theft. My testimony is based largely on our recent reports on tax noncompliance and updates our 2011 testimonies on the tax gap and identity theft. 2 Additional information on our scope and methodology is available in our published products.

This testimony and the reports and testimonies upon which it is based were conducted in accordance with generally accepted government auditing standards. Those standards require that we plan and perform the audit to obtain sufficient, appropriate evidence to provide a reasonable basis for our findings and conclusions based on our audit objectives. We believe that the evidence obtained provides a reasonable basis for our findings and conclusions based on our audit objectives.

For this hearing, we updated prior reported information about the estimated amounts for various components of the 2006 tax gap, the data and methodology used to estimate the 2006 tax gap, and actions IRS has taken to address our recommendations to improve taxpayer compliance. We confirmed the new information with IRS officials.

# THE TAX GAP IS SPREAD ACROSS VARIOUS TYPES OF TAXPAYERS AND TAXES

## Characteristics of the Tax Gap

The gross tax gap has grown in dollar terms since IRS's previous estimate for tax year 2001, increasing from $345 billion to $450 billion for tax year 2006.[3] However, given the growth of the economy and total federal tax liability over that period, the percentage of taxes owed that taxpayers paid voluntarily and on time, known as the voluntary compliance rate, has remained relatively constant—83.7 percent in 2001 and 83.1 percent in 2006.[4]

The tax gap estimate is an aggregate of estimates for the three primary types of noncompliance: (1) underreporting of tax liabilities on tax returns; (2) underpayment of taxes due from filed returns; and (3) nonfiling, which refers to the failure to file a required tax return altogether or on time.[5] The estimate also covers the five types of taxes that IRS administers— individual income, corporate income, employment, estate, and excise taxes.

The tax gap includes unintentional errors as well as intentional evasion, such as intentionally underreporting income, intentionally over-reporting expenses, and engaging in abusive tax shelters or frivolous tax schemes. It does not include legal tax avoidance activities (legally lowering tax liability), taxes due from illegally derived income, or various forms of fraud. For example, in general, refund fraud related to identity theft would not be included in the tax gap estimate because it does not involve evading a tax liability. Nevertheless, as discussed later in the testimony, actions taken to improve overall compliance and reduce the tax gap could also potentially address identity theft related fraud.

**Table 1. IRS's Tax Year 2006 Gross Tax Gap Estimates by Type of Noncompliance and Type of Tax**

| Dollars in billions | | | | | | |
|---|---|---|---|---|---|---|
| | | | Type of tax | | | |
| Type of noncompliance | Individual income tax | Corporate income tax | Employment tax | Estate tax | Excise tax | Total |
| Underreporting | $235 | $67 | $72 | $2 | No estimate | $376 |
| Underpayment | 36 | 4 | 4 | 2 | 0.1 | 46 |
| Nonfiling | 25 | No estimate | No estimate | 3 | No estimate | 28 |
| Total | $296 | $71 | $76 | $7 | $0.1 | $450 |

Source: IRS.

A critical step toward reducing the tax gap is to understand the sources and nature of taxpayer noncompliance. As shown in table 1, noncompliance does not come from a single source but rather occurs across different types of taxes and taxpayers. For example, individual income tax accounted for most of the tax gap estimate for tax year 2006. However, corporate income tax and employment tax also contributed a significant portion.

As shown in table 2, individual income tax underreporting includes both nonbusiness income tax and business income tax underreporting. Business income for individuals includes income from a variety of business types, including sole proprietors,[6] partnerships, and S corporations,[7] many of which are small businesses. Nearly 40 percent, or $179 billion, of the 2006 gross tax gap can be attributed to these types of business taxpayers who underreport their business income tax, and by extension their self-employment tax, on their individual income tax returns.[8] Further, the misreporting of business income tax can take on a variety of forms.

**Table 2. Underreporting Portion of IRS's Tax Year 2006 Gross Tax Gap Estimates**

| Dollars in billions | |
|---|---|
| Tax gap component | Estimated underreporting amount |
| Individual income tax | $235 |
| Nonbusiness income | 68 |
| Business income | 122 |
| Adjustments, deductions, and exemptions | 17 |
| Credits | 28 |
| | |
| Corporate income tax | $67 |
| Small corporations | 19 |
| Large corporations | 48 |
| | |
| Employment tax | $72 |
| Self-employment tax | 57 |
| FICA and unemployment tax | 15 |
| | |
| Estate tax | $2 |
| | |
| Total underreporting | $376 |

Source: IRS.

For example, misreporting of non-corporate business income tax can be largely attributed to sole proprietors who understated receipts or overstated expenses.[9] A key reason for this misreporting is well known. Unlike wage and some investment income, sole proprietors' income is not subject to withholding and only a portion is subject to information reporting to IRS by third parties.

As shown in figure 1, the extent to which individual taxpayers accurately report their income is related to the extent to which the income is reported to them and IRS by third parties or taxes on the income are withheld. For example, for types of income for which there is little or no information reporting, such as business income, individual taxpayers tend to misreport over half of their income. In contrast, employers report most wages, salaries, and tip compensation to employees and IRS through Form W-2. Also, banks and other financial institutions provide information returns (Forms 1099) to account holders and IRS showing the taxpayers' annual income from some types of investments. Findings from IRS's study of individual tax compliance indicate that nearly 99 percent of these types of income are accurately reported on individual tax returns.

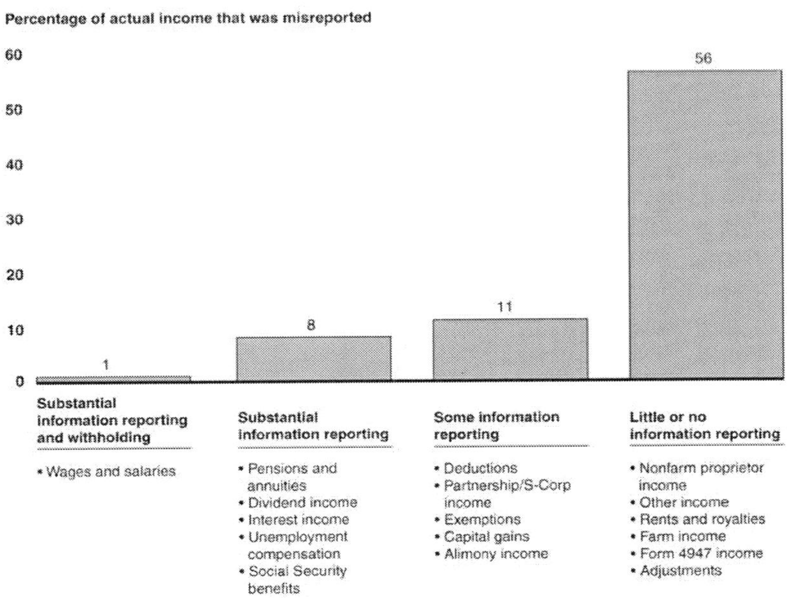


Source: IRS.

Figure 1. Effect of Information Reporting on Taxpayer Compliance, Tax Year 2006.

Taxpayers misreport income and expenses for a variety of reasons. Some misreporting is intentional; some is unintentional. Often it is impossible to tell from a tax return whether errors are intentional or unintentional or even who made the error. For example, paid tax return preparers could make errors or taxpayers could fail to share relevant information with their preparers. Our past reports shed some light on the extent of unintentional errors. In our report on securities cost basis reporting,[10] we found that among individual taxpayers who misreported securities sales, roughly one-third over-reported income (i.e., they overstated gains or understated losses).11 For sole proprietors, we reported that 9 percent over-reported their net income, while 61 percent underreported their net income in 2001.12 It seems likely that such instances of over-reporting could be due to unintentional errors.

## Measuring the Tax Gap

We have long encouraged regular tax gap measurement because these estimates are important to gauge progress in addressing the tax gap and, perhaps more importantly, because analyzing the data used to estimate it can help identify ways to improve tax compliance.

One source of such data is the National Research Program (NRP), which uses audits of a stratified, random sample of tax returns to produce statistically valid estimates of noncompliance for the entire population of tax return filers. IRS uses the NRP sample results to better target its enforcement examinations of noncompliant taxpayers. Better targeting examinations to taxpayers who are noncompliant reduces burden on compliant taxpayers.

Updated compliance data can also help identify changes in tax laws and regulations that may improve compliance. For example, we analyzed NRP data on individual taxpayer compliance and reported that, among other things, Congress could consider requiring brokers to report to both taxpayers and IRS the adjusted basis of securities that taxpayers sell.[13] Congress enacted this provision,[14] which the Joint Committee on Taxation estimated would raise $6.7 billion in revenue through 2018.

As we have reported in the past, closing the entire gap may not be feasible since it could entail more intrusive recordkeeping or reporting than the public is willing to accept or more resources than IRS is able to commit. 15 However, given the size of the tax gap, even modest reductions would yield very significant financial benefits. We have made numerous recommendations over time that could address the tax gap, as follows.

# VARIOUS STRATEGIES ARE REQUIRED TO REDUCE THE TAX GAP

Multiple approaches are needed to reduce the tax gap. No single approach is likely to fully and cost-effectively address noncompliance since the noncompliance has multiple causes and spans different types of taxes and taxpayers.

While the tax gap will remain a challenge into the future, the following strategies could help. These strategies would require actions by Congress or IRS.

## Enhancing Information Reporting by Third Parties to IRS

Information reporting is a powerful tool that reduces tax evasion and helps taxpayers comply voluntarily. Several major new information requirements have recently taken effect, based at least in part on our work and recommendations.

- Brokers are required to report their clients' basis for securities sales, starting in 2012.[16]
- Banks and other third parties are required to report businesses' credit card and similar receipts, starting in 2011.[17]
- Under the Foreign Account Tax Compliance Act, starting in 2014, U.S. financial institutions and other entities are required to withhold a portion of certain payments made to foreign financial institutions that have not entered into an agreement with IRS to report details on U.S. account holders to IRS.[18]

As these three sets of information reporting requirements have only recently taken effect, it is too soon to tell the actual impact they are having on taxpayer compliance.

We have identified other options for information reporting.

- *Service payments to corporations.* Currently, businesses must report to IRS payments for services they make to unincorporated persons or businesses, but payments to corporations generally do not have to be reported.[19]

- *Service payments made by landlords.* Taxpayers who rent out real estate are required to report to IRS expense payments for certain services, such as payments for property repairs, only if their rental activity is considered a trade or business. However, the law does not clearly spell out how to determine when rental real estate activity is considered a trade or business.[20]

Broader requirements for these two forms of information reporting, covering goods in addition to services, were enacted into law in 2010 but were later repealed.

We believe the more narrow extensions of information reporting to include services, but not goods, remain important options for improving compliance.

Additionally, we have identified existing information reporting requirements that could be enhanced.

- *Higher education expenses.* Eligible educational institutions are currently required to report information on qualified tuition and related expenses for higher education so that taxpayers can determine the amount of educational tax benefits they can claim.[21] IRS revising the information reporting form could improve the usefulness of reported information.[22]
- *Mortgaged properties.* Requiring third parties, such as mortgage lenders, to report mortgaged property addresses in addition to information they are already required to report on mortgaged properties would help IRS identify potential noncompliance.[23]

Identifying additional third-party reporting opportunities is challenging. Considerations include whether any third parties have accurate information available in a timely manner, the burden of reporting on the third parties, and whether IRS can enforce the reporting requirement. To illustrate, in a 2009 report, we found that a major reason why little information reporting on sole proprietor expenses exists is because of the difficulty identifying third parties.[24]

For example, there is no third party that could verify the business use of cars or trucks by sole proprietors.

## Ensuring High-Quality Services to Taxpayers

Ensuring high-quality taxpayer services, such as by telephone and correspondence or online, can help taxpayers who wish to comply with tax laws but do not understand their obligations. However, in recent years and continuing this year, IRS's service performance has seen declines. Tax law changes and other funding priorities have affected IRS's ability to provide quality taxpayer services. For example, we recently reported that call volume has increased nearly 35 percent from the same time period last year, which IRS attributed, in part, to taxpayer questions about tax law changes.[25] Concurrently, taxpayers' ability to get through to IRS telephone assistors has declined.[26]

Through late February of this year, 65 percent of callers seeking to talk to an IRS telephone assistor got through, compared to 70 percent for 2011. To improve service, we have recommended that IRS determine the costs and benefits of creating additional automated telephone applications and finalize a more comprehensive plan for online services, including an assessment of granting taxpayers the ability to update their account information online.

## Devoting Additional Resources to Enforcement

Devoting additional resources to enforcement would enable IRS to contact millions of potentially noncompliant taxpayers that it currently identifies but cannot contact given resource constraints.

However, determining the appropriate level of enforcement resources to provide IRS requires taking into account factors such as how effectively and efficiently IRS is currently using its resources, how to strike the proper balance between IRS's taxpayer service and enforcement activities, and competing federal funding priorities.

For example, in a 2009 report, we found that despite investing nearly a quarter of all revenue agent time in 2008, IRS was able to examine (audit) about 1 percent of estimated noncompliant sole proprietors.

Not only are these exams burdensome for businesses, they are also costly for IRS and yield less revenue than examinations of other categories of taxpayers, in part because most sole proprietorships are small in terms of receipts.[27]

## Expanding Compliance Checks before IRS Issues Refunds

IRS could reduce the tax gap by expanding compliance checks before issuing refunds to taxpayers. The Commissioner of Internal Revenue has talked about a long-term vision to increase compliance activities before refunds are sent to taxpayers. In one example, IRS is exploring a requirement that third parties send information returns to IRS and taxpayers at the same time as opposed to the current requirement that some information returns go to taxpayers before going to IRS. The intent is to allow IRS to match those information returns to tax returns during tax return filing season rather than after the filing season is complete.[28] As will be discussed later, this approach could also help IRS address identity theft-related fraud and could also allow IRS to use its enforcement resources on other significant compliance problems. However, the Commissioner made clear that his vision for more prerefund compliance checks will take considerable time to implement, will require a major reworking of some fundamental IRS computer systems, and could impose some additional burden on third parties.

## Leveraging External Resources Such as Paid Tax Return Preparers and Whistleblowers

Another way IRS may be able to reduce the tax gap is by leveraging external resources.

- Paid tax return preparers prepare approximately 60 percent of all tax returns filed, and IRS has acknowledged that paid preparers' actions have an enormous impact on its ability to administer tax laws effectively. Based in part on our work and recommendations, IRS recently developed new requirements for paid preparers, such as competency testing, which it has concluded will increase tax compliance.[29] IRS's goals for the program include leveraging relationships with paid preparers and improving the accuracy of the tax returns they prepare.
- Tax whistleblowers can help improve tax compliance by providing information to IRS on others' suspected tax noncompliance. We have made several recommendations for IRS to improve its whistleblower program through enhanced data collection and whistleblower claim

processing timeliness.[30] According to IRS, it is in the process of implementing these recommendations.

## Modernizing Information Systems

Modernization of IRS's information systems could improve taxpayer compliance. IRS is engaged in a multiyear effort to replace the systems it uses to process individual tax returns and receive electronically filed tax returns.[31] IRS had identified various compliance benefits to replacing the system it uses to process individual tax returns, including increasing taxpayer and paid preparer voluntary compliance and examination case selection.[32] Among other benefits, replacing its electronic filing system will allow IRS to accept taxpayers' prior-year returns and portable document format (PDF) files attached to their tax returns. According to IRS officials, posting more comprehensive information from individual income tax returns to its computer systems could facilitate the examination process, expedite taxpayer contacts for faster resolution, and potentially better define specific tax gap issues.[33]

## Simplifying the Tax Code or Fundamental Tax Reform

Tax code complexity can lead to noncompliance. Efforts to simplify or reform the tax code may help reduce the tax gap by making it easier for individuals and businesses to understand and voluntarily comply with their tax obligations. For example, eliminating or combining tax expenditures, such as exemptions, deductions, and credits, could help taxpayers reduce unintentional errors and limit opportunities for tax evasion.

Policymakers may find it useful to compare any proposed changes to the tax code based on a set of widely accepted criteria for assessing alternative tax proposals. These criteria include the equity, or fairness, of the tax system; the economic efficiency, or neutrality, of the system; and the simplicity, transparency, and administrability of the system. These criteria can sometimes conflict, and the weight one places on each criterion will vary among individuals. Our publication, *Understanding the Tax Reform Debate: Background, Criteria, & Questions*, may be useful in guiding policymakers as they consider tax reform proposals.[34] Our recent reports show how changing tax laws to include more consistent definitions across tax provisions could help taxpayers more easily understand and comply with their obligations.

- For example, higher education expenses that qualify for some of the savings and credit provisions in the tax code differ by provision. These dissimilar definitions require that taxpayers keep track of expenses separately, applying some expenses to some tax preferences but not others.[35]
- Likewise, more clarity would help taxpayers determine how to treat certain financial derivative products for tax purposes. Unique characteristics of financial derivatives make them particularly difficult for the tax code and IRS to address. Deferring gains or accelerating losses, changing ordinary income into capital gains or vice versa for losses, and altering the source of gains to avoid withholding taxes are examples of inconsistent tax rules for financial derivatives resulting in equivalent economic outcomes being taxed differently.[36]

## CHALLENGES TO ADDRESSING IDENTITY THEFT

Identity theft creates problems for both taxpayers and IRS. In refund fraud cases, an identity thief uses a legitimate taxpayer's identity to fraudulently file a tax return and claim a refund during the filing season. In these cases, the identity thief typically uses a stolen Social Security Number (SSN) to file a forged tax return and obtain a refund early in the filing season. The legitimate owner of the SSN may not be aware that this has occurred until he or she files a tax return later in the filing season and IRS discovers that two returns have been filed using the same SSN. In this instance, the legitimate taxpayer's refund will likely be frozen until IRS can determine the legitimate owner of the SSN.[37]

In our June 2011 testimony before this subcommittee, we reported that IRS faced various challenges in resolving, detecting, and preventing identity theft. These challenges included limitations in coordinating with other agencies and taxpayers because of privacy and other laws, inability to detect suspicious cases until after fraud has occurred, and the lack of resources and authority to investigate and prosecute identity thieves.[38]

Addressing these challenges will require significant, long-term changes in IRS's operations and systems. As previously discussed, the Commissioner's long-term vision to increase up-front compliance activities could help. For example, matching employer information with tax returns before refunds are issued could prevent identity thieves from using phony W-2s to claim fraudulent refunds. However, significant changes would be needed before this matching could occur. Third-party information returns would need to be filed with IRS earlier in the filing season.[39] IRS would also need to improve its automated processing systems; IRS's current Customer Account Data Engine (CADE 2) effort is one key step.[40]

Chairman Platts, Ranking Member Towns, and Members of the Subcommittee, this completes my prepared statement. I would be pleased to respond to any questions that you may have at this time.

## APPENDIX I: 2006 TAX GAP ESTIMATE DATA AND METHODOLOGY

The Internal Revenue Service's (IRS) tax gap estimates are based on a variety of data sources and methodologies. For example, IRS studied individual taxpayer compliance through the National Research Program (NRP) and used the resulting compliance data to estimate the tax gap for individual income tax underreporting and the portion of employment tax underreporting attributed to self-employment taxes for tax year 2006.

The 2006 Individual NRP involved auditing a random selection of about 13,000 to 14,000 individual tax returns and is much smaller than the tax year 2001 Individual NRP of approximately 45,000 returns. Starting with the 2006 Individual NRP compliance study, IRS is using a rolling sample, which will combine samples across three years. According to IRS, this change will reduce cost and provide more up to date compliance data. The sample design for the 2006 Individual NRP included 11 primary strata, which were based on the examination classes used in audit workload selection. Also, the 2006 Individual NRP was designed to oversample returns with business income reported on Schedule C, E, or F or Form 2106.

The individual underreporting gap for tax year 2006 was based on findings from the 2006 Individual NRP and from an econometric analysis of tax year 2001 NRP data. This econometric analysis, called Detection-Controlled Estimation (DCE), attempts to account for income that taxpayers do not report on their tax returns and that NRP auditors could not detect. Because insufficient NRP data has been accumulated for tax year 2006 and later years for full DCE analysis, an improved DCE was undertaken using tax year 2001 NRP data and adjusted using other information to estimate undetected income for tax year 2006 NRP returns.

We have not verified the accuracy of IRS's estimate of the tax gap. According to IRS, a significant portion of IRS's 2006 tax gap estimate is based on recent compliance data and improved estimation methods. However, the tax gap estimate continues to be incomplete and partly based on older data. For example, the underreporting estimates for both FICA and unemployment taxes are projections based on applying the estimated compliance rates for 1984 to currently reported taxes.

To estimate the 2006 individual nonfiling gap, IRS used tax year 2005 third-party information returns, rather than the Census Exact Match study, as it did for the tax year 2001 estimate. The underpayment component of the tax gap is not an estimate but rather represents the actual tax amounts that taxpayers reported on time, but did not pay on time.

## End Notes

[1] Throughout this statement, references to the tax gap refer to the gross tax gap unless otherwise noted.

[2] GAO, Tax Gap: Complexity and Taxpayer Compliance, GAO-11-747T (Washington, D.C.: June 28, 2011), and Taxes and Identity Theft: Status of IRS Initiatives to Help Victimized Taxpayers, GAO-11-721T (Washington, D.C.: June 2, 2011).

[3] These amounts have not been adjusted for inflation.

[4] This 30 percent increase in the size of the gross tax gap from 2001 to 2006 is similar to the increase in the size of the United States economy (gross domestic product) over the time period. Likewise, total tax liabilities increased nearly 26 percent, from about $2.1 trillion to about $2.7 trillion, from tax years 2001 to 2006. (Dollar amounts for total tax liabilities do not match percentage increase because of rounding.) IRS also estimated that corporate income tax underreporting increased by $37 billion during this time. However, this growth may not indicate increased corporate noncompliance. According to IRS, the 2001 estimate of this portion of the tax gap was estimated based on old empirical data and was likely understated. In addition, from 2001 to 2006, corporation income tax liabilities more than doubled, while individual income tax liabilities grew by 15 percent.

[5] Taxpayers who receive filing extensions, pay their full tax liability by payment due dates, and file returns prior to extension deadlines are considered to have filed on time.

[6] Sole proprietors are self-employed individuals who should file a Schedule C with their individual tax returns to report profits and losses from their businesses. Sole proprietors include those who provide services, such as doctors or accountants; produce goods, such as manufacturers; and sell goods at fixed locations, such as car dealers and grocers.

[7] S corporations provide limited liability protection to shareholders and "pass through" gains and losses to shareholders' individual tax returns without generally paying taxes at the entity level. Limited liability protection means that a shareholder's financial liability for a company is limited to the amount of their investment in the company. Owners of S corporations are referred to as shareholders.

[8] Self-employed individuals are generally required to calculate and remit Social Security and Medicare taxes to the U.S. Treasury each quarter. As employment taxes and income taxes for self-employed taxpayers are largely assessed on the same income, self-employed individuals who underreport their income consequently underreport the employment tax due on that income.

[9] GAO, Tax Gap: A Strategy for Reducing the Gap Should Include Options for Addressing Sole Proprietor Noncompliance, GAO-07-1014 (Washington, D.C.: July 13, 2007).

[10] Generally, a taxpayer's gain or loss from a securities sale is simply the difference between the gross proceeds from the sale and the original purchase price, or original cost basis. However, before taxpayers can determine any gains or losses from securities sales, they must determine if and how the original cost basis of the securities must be adjusted to reflect certain events, such as stock splits, nontaxable dividends, or nondividend distributions.

[11] GAO, Capital Gains Tax Gap: Requiring Brokers to Report Securities Cost Basis Would Improve Compliance if Related Challenges Are Addressed, GAO-06-603 (Washington, D.C.: June 13, 2006).

[12] GAO-07-1014. 13GAO-06-603.

[14] Energy Improvement and Extension Act of 2008, Pub. L. No 110-343, § 403, 122 Stat. 3768, 3854 (Oct. 3, 2008).

[15] GAO, Taxpayer Compliance: Analyzing the Nature of the Income Tax Gap, GAO/T-GGD-97-35 (Washington, D.C.: Jan. 9, 1997).

[16] GAO-06-603.

[17] GAO, Tax Administration: Costs and Uses of Third-Party Information Returns, GAO-08-266 (Washington, D.C.: Nov. 20, 2007).

[18] GAO, Reporting Foreign Accounts to IRS: Extent of Duplication Not Currently Known, but Requirements Can Be Clarified, GAO-12-403 (Washington, D.C.: Feb 28, 2012).

[19] GAO, Tax Gap: IRS Could Do More to Promote Compliance by Third Parties with Miscellaneous Income Reporting Requirements, GAO-09-238 (Washington, D.C.: Jan. 28, 2009).

[20] GAO, Tax Gap: Actions That Could Improve Rental Real Estate Reporting Compliance, GAO-08-956 (Washington, D.C.: Aug. 28, 2008).

[21] 26 U.S.C. § 6050S.

[22] GAO, 2009 Tax Filing Season: IRS Met Many 2009 Goals, but Telephone Access Remained Low, and Taxpayer Service and Enforcement Could Be Improved, GAO-10-225 (Washington, D.C.: Dec. 10, 2009).

[23] GAO, Home Mortgage Interest Deduction: Despite Challenges Presented by Complex Tax Rules, IRS Could Enhance Enforcement and Guidance, GAO-09-769 (Washington, D.C.: July 29, 2009); Tax Administration: Expanded Information Reporting Could Help IRS Address Compliance Challenges with Forgiven Mortgage Debt, GAO-10-997 (Washington, D.C.: Aug 31, 2010); and GAO-08-956.

[24] GAO, Tax Gap: Limiting Sole Proprietor Loss Deductions Could Improve Compliance but Would Also Limit Some Legitimate Losses, GAO-09-815 (Washington, D.C.: Sept. 10, 2009).

[25] GAO, 2011 Filing Season: Processing Gains, but Assistance Could Be Enhanced by More Self-Service Tools, GAO-12-176 (Washington, D.C.: Dec. 15, 2011).

[26] GAO, Internal Revenue Service: Interim Results of 2012 Tax Filing Season and Summary of the Fiscal Year 2013 Budget Request, GAO-12-566 (Washington, D.C.: Mar. 20, 2012).

[27] GAO-09-815.

[28] GAO, Taxpayer Account Strategy: IRS Should Finish Defining Benefits and Improve Cost Estimates, GAO-11-168 (Washington, D.C.: Mar. 24, 2011).

[29] GAO, Tax Preparer Regulation: IRS Needs a Documented Framework to Achieve Goal of Improving Taxpayer Compliance, GAO-11-336 (Washington, D.C.: Mar. 31, 2011); Tax Preparers: Oregon's Regulatory Regime May Lead to Improved Federal Tax Return Accuracy and Provides a Possible Model for National Regulation, GAO-08-781 (Washington, D.C.: Aug. 15, 2008); and Internal Revenue Service: Fiscal Year 2009 Budget Request and Interim Performance Results of IRS's 2008 Tax Filing Season, GAO-08-567 (Washington, D.C.: Mar. 13, 2008).

[30] GAO, Tax Whistleblowers: Incomplete Data Hinders IRS's Ability to Manage Claim Processing Time and Enhance External Communication, GAO-11-683 (Washington, D.C.: Aug. 10, 2011).

[31] GAO-12-176. 32GAO-11-168.

[33] GAO, Tax Administration: 2007 Filing Season Continues Trend of Improvement, but Opportunities to Reduce Costs and Increase Tax Compliance Should be Evaluated, GAO-08-38 (Washington, D.C.: Nov. 15, 2007).

[34] GAO, Understanding the Tax Reform Debate: Background, Criteria, & Questions, GAO-05-1009SP (Washington, D.C.: September 2005).

[35] GAO, Student Aid and Postsecondary Tax Preferences: Limited Research Exists on Effectiveness of Tools to Assist Students and Families through Title IV Student Aid and Tax Preferences, GAO-05-684 (Washington, D.C.: July 29, 2005).

[36] GAO, Financial Derivatives: Disparate Tax Treatment and Information Gaps Create Uncertainty and Potential Abuse, GAO-11-750 (Washington, D.C.: Sept. 20, 2011).

[37] Identity theft may also involve employment fraud. This occurs when an identity thief uses someone else's name and SSN to obtain a job. In this instance, IRS would receive a Form W-2 or a Form 1099 reporting income on the taxpayer's account, which the rightful owner of the SSN had not earned and does not report as income to IRS. As a result, the taxpayer may be subject to enforcement action when, during the filing process, IRS matches what the employer and the taxpayer report and it appears that he or she earned more income than was reported on his or her tax return.

[38] GAO, Tax Administration: IRS Has Implemented Initiatives to Prevent, Detect, and Resolve Identity Theft-Related Problems, but Needs to Assess Their Effectiveness, GAO-09-882 (Washington, D.C.: Sept. 8, 2009), and GAO-11-721T.

[39] Many information returns, such as forms W-2 filed by employers, are not due to the government until the end of February.

[40] GAO-11-18.

In: Tax Gaps
Editor: Rondell Meinke
ISBN: 978-1-62417-452-0


*Chapter 5*

# TAX GAP: COMPLEXITY AND TAXPAYER COMPLIANCE. STATEMENT OF MICHAEL BROSTEK, DIRECTOR, TAX ISSUES, STRATEGIC ISSUES, GOVERNMENT ACCOUNTABILITY OFFICE. HEARING ON "COMPLEXITY AND THE TAX GAP: MAKING TAX COMPLIANCE EASIER AND COLLECTING WHAT'S DUE"*

*United States Government Accountability Office*

## WHY GAO DID THIS STUDY

Taxes are necessary because they fund the services provided by government. Several years ago, the Internal Revenue Service (IRS) estimated that the gross tax gap—the difference between taxes owed and taxes paid on time—was $345 billion for 2001. In the face of large and growing deficits, it is important to seek out potential causes and solutions to the tax gap.

* This is an edited, reformatted and augmented version of The United States Government Accountability Office publication GAO-11-747T Presented June 28, 2011 before the Senate Finance Committee.

Achieving high levels of voluntary compliance is made more challenging as the tax code expands. Tax expenditures—preferential provisions in the code such as exemptions, exclusions, deductions, credits, and deferral of tax liability— have expanded the tax code, more than doubling in number since 1974.

GAO's statement focuses on four key areas: (1) how complexity adds to taxpayer burden and economic efficiency costs; (2) how complexities in reporting income contribute to the tax gap; (3) how tax expenditures add complexity and contribute to the tax gap; and (4) possible strategies for addressing the tax gap. The statement is based largely on GAO's previous work conducted on tax compliance issues affecting individual taxpayers from 2005 through 2011.

## What GAO Recommends

GAO does not make any new recommendations in this testimony.

## What GAO Found

The federal tax system contains complex rules. These rules may be necessary, for example, to ensure proper measurement of income, target benefits to specific taxpayers, and address areas of noncompliance. However, these complex rules also impose a wide range of recordkeeping, planning, computational, and filing requirements upon businesses and individuals. Complying with these requirements costs taxpayers time and money. In 2005 GAO reviewed existing studies and reported that even using the lowest available compliance cost estimates for the personal and corporate income tax, combined compliance costs would total $107 billion (roughly 1 percent of gross domestic product) per year; other studies estimate costs 1.5 times as large. Economic efficiency costs, which are reductions in economic well-being caused by changes in behavior due to taxes, are estimated to be even larger.

Although many taxpayers have simple forms of income, others do not—especially those who receive income from capital gains, rents, self-employment, and other sources—and they may be required to do complicated calculations and keep detailed records. This complexity can engender errors and underpaid taxes. For example, GAO has documented millions of taxpayer errors in following complex rules for determining taxpayers' "basis"—

generally the taxpayer's investment in a property—in securities they sold or corporations they own.

Tax expenditures add to tax code complexity in part because they require taxpayers to learn about, determine their eligibility for, and choose between tax expenditures that have similar purposes. Tax expenditures also complicate tax planning, as taxpayers must predict their own future circumstances as well as future tax rules to make the best choice among provisions. Taxpayer errors contribute to the tax gap. For example, in 2001 taxpayers underreported $6.3 billion in net income due to misreported Individual Retirement Arrangement (IRA) distributions. But taxpayers also may underclaim benefits to which they are entitled. According to GAO's past analysis, of tax filers who appeared to be eligible for a higher-education tax credit or tuition deduction in tax year 2005, about 19 percent, representing about 412,000 returns, failed to claim any of them.

No single approach is likely to fully and cost-effectively address the tax gap, but several strategies could improve taxpayer compliance. These strategies could require actions by Congress or IRS. For example, Congress can simplify the tax code by eliminating some tax expenditures and by making definitions more consistent across the tax code. IRS and Congress could take steps to enhance information reporting by third parties or expand compliance checking before refunds are issued.

Chairman Baucus, Ranking Member Hatch, and Members of the Committee,

I am pleased to be here today to discuss complexity in the tax code, taxpayer burden, and steps to improve compliance. Taxes are necessary because they fund the services provided by government. Complexity, and the lack of transparency that it can create, exacerbate doubts about the current tax system's fairness. Public confidence in the nation's tax laws and tax administration is critical because we rely heavily on a system of voluntary compliance. If taxpayers do not have confidence in the tax system or do not believe that it is easy to understand and treats everyone fairly, then voluntary compliance is likely to decline.

The current tax system is widely viewed as complex, thereby reducing the ability of individuals to understand and comply with tax laws. According to a 2010 report by the National Taxpayer Advocate, the tax code has grown so long that it has become challenging even to figure out how long it is. Important sources of tax code complexity are income documentation requirements and tax expenditure rules, which I will discuss in more detail later in my statement.

Several years ago, the Internal Revenue Service (IRS) estimated that the gross tax gap—the difference between taxes owed and taxes paid on time—was $345 billion in 2001. We have said in past testimonies that there are no easy fixes to this problem. But in the face of large and growing structural deficits, it is nevertheless important that the government continues to seek out potential causes and solutions. This is in keeping with another theme that we have emphasized: that fundamental reexamination of government programs, policies, and priorities is necessary to assure that they match the needs of the 21st century. While we do not know the extent to which tax code complexity contributes to the tax gap, this hearing is an important step as Congress considers the role played by tax code complexity in either contributing to the tax gap or impeding progress towards solutions.

My statement today will cover (1) how complexity adds to taxpayer burden and economic efficiency costs; (2) how complexities in reporting income contribute to the tax gap; (3) how tax expenditures[1] add complexity and contribute to the tax gap; and (4) possible strategies for addressing the tax gap. It is based mostly on our work from 2005 through 2011 on tax compliance issues affecting individual taxpayers. Those performance audits were conducted in accordance with generally accepted government auditing standards. Those standards require that we plan and perform the audit to obtain sufficient, appropriate evidence to provide a reasonable basis for our findings and conclusions based on our audit objectives. We believe that the evidence obtained provided a reasonable basis for our findings and conclusions based on our audit objectives.

We have also updated our analyses from our previous work on the number and sum of tax expenditure provisions.[2] To determine the reliability of this data, we reviewed related documentation and tested data for obvious errors. We determined that the data were sufficiently reliable for the purposes of this testimony.

## BACKGROUND

### Tax Gap

The gross tax gap is an estimate of the difference between the taxes—including individual income, corporate income, employment, estate, and excise taxes—that should have been paid voluntarily and on time and what was actually paid for a specific year.[3] Of the estimated $345 billion tax gap for tax year 2001, IRS estimated that it would eventually recover about $55 billion of that through late payments and enforcement actions, for a net tax gap of $290 billion. The estimate is an aggregate of estimates for the three primary types of noncompliance: (1) underreporting of tax liabilities on tax returns; (2) underpayment of taxes due from filed returns; and (3) nonfiling, which refers to the failure to file a required tax return altogether or on time.[4] We have made many recommendations over time that could address the tax gap.[5]

IRS's tax gap estimates for each type of noncompliance include estimates for some or all of the five types of taxes that IRS administers. Underreporting of tax liabilities can occur when a taxpayer underreports income earned or overclaims deductions from income. As shown in table 1, underreporting of tax liabilities—particularly for the individual income tax—accounted for most of the tax gap estimate for tax year 2001. We have encouraged regular tax gap measurements, and IRS officials have indicated that they will be updating their tax gap estimates later in 2011 or early 2012. We believe that these estimates are important to gauge progress in addressing the tax gap and because analyzing the data used to estimate it can help identify ways to improve tax compliance.

**Table 1. IRS's Tax Year 2001 Gross Tax Gap Estimates by Type of Noncompliance and Type of Tax**

| Dollars in billions | | | | | | |
|---|---|---|---|---|---|---|
| | | | Type of tax | | | |
| Type of noncompliance | Individual income tax | Corporate income tax | Employment tax | Estate tax | Excise tax | Total |
| Underreporting | $197 | $30 | $54 | $4 | No | $285 |
| Underpayment | 23 | 2 | 5 | 2 | 1 | 34 |
| Nonfiling | 25 | No | No estimate | 2 | No | 27 |
| Total | $244 | $32 | $59 | $8 | $1 | $345 |

Source: IRS.

Note: Some figures do not sum to totals because of rounding.

Taxpayers who underreported the amount of individual income tax they owed represented an estimated $197 billion of the 2001 tax gap, and $165 billion of that amount was due to individual tax filers underreporting their income. As shown in table 2, underreporting of individuals' business income and nonbusiness income accounted for $109 billion and $56 billion, respectively, of the 2001 tax gap.

**Table 2. Components of the Tax Gap for Individual Income Tax Underreporting, Tax Year 2001**

| Type of income or offset | Tax gap amount (dollars in billions) | Net misreporting percentage |
|---|---|---|
| Business income | $109 | 43% |
| Nonbusiness income | 56 | 4 |
| Credits | 17 | 26 |
| Deductions | 14 | 5 |
| Exemptions | 4 | 5 |
| Adjustments | -3 | -21 |
| Total | $197 | 18% |

Source: IRS.

Note: Figures may not sum to totals because of rounding. Net misreporting percentage is the net amount misreported on a given line item or category expressed as a percentage of the sum of the absolute values of the amounts that should have been reported for that item or category.

IRS has concerns with the certainty of the tax gap estimate for tax year 2001 in part because some areas of the 2001 estimate rely on data originally gathered in the 1970s and 1980s. IRS has no estimates for other areas of the tax gap, and it is inherently difficult to measure some types of noncompliance.[6] Some analysts believe the 2001 estimate likely underestimated the tax gap and that in absolute dollars it is likely larger now than in 2001.

IRS's overall approach to reducing the tax gap consists of improving service to taxpayers and enhancing enforcement of the tax laws. IRS seeks to improve voluntary compliance through efforts such as education and outreach programs and tax form simplification. It also uses its enforcement authority to ensure that taxpayers are reporting and paying the proper amounts of taxes through efforts such as examining tax returns and matching the amount of income taxpayers report on their tax returns to the income amounts reported on information returns[7] it receives from third parties. In spite of IRS's efforts to improve taxpayer compliance, the rate at which taxpayers pay their taxes voluntarily and on time has tended to range from around 81 percent to around 84 percent over the past three decades.

## Tax Expenditures

The sum of the estimated revenue loss due to tax expenditures was over $1 trillion in 2010.[8] Tax expenditures are often aimed at policy goals similar to those of federal spending programs. Existing tax expenditures, for example, help students and families finance higher education and provide incentives for people to save for retirement. Because tax expenditures result in forgone revenue for the government, they have a significant effect on overall tax rates—all else equal, for any given level of revenue, tax expenditures mean that overall tax rates must be higher than a tax system with no tax expenditures. In 2005, we recommended that the federal government take several steps to ensure greater transparency of and accountability for tax expenditures by reporting better information on tax expenditure performance and more fully incorporating tax expenditures into federal performance management and budget review processes.[9]

# Complexity Can Have Value, but Adds to Compliance and Efficiency Costs

The federal tax system contains complex rules. These rules may be necessary, for example, to ensure proper measurement of income, target benefits to specific taxpayers, and address areas of noncompliance.

However, these complex rules also impose a wide range of record keeping, planning, computational, and filing requirements upon businesses and individuals. Complying with these requirements costs taxpayers time and money. As shown in figure 1, these costs to taxpayers are above and beyond what they pay to the government in taxes.

Estimating total compliance costs is difficult because neither the government nor taxpayers maintain regular accounts of these costs, and federal tax requirements often overlap with record keeping and reporting that taxpayers do for other purposes. Although available estimates are uncertain, taken together, they suggest that total compliance costs are large. For example, in 2005 we reviewed existing studies and reported that even using the lowest available compliance cost estimates for the personal and corporate income tax, combined compliance costs would total $107 billion (roughly 1 percent of gross domestic product [GDP]) per year; other studies estimate costs 1.5 times as large.[10]

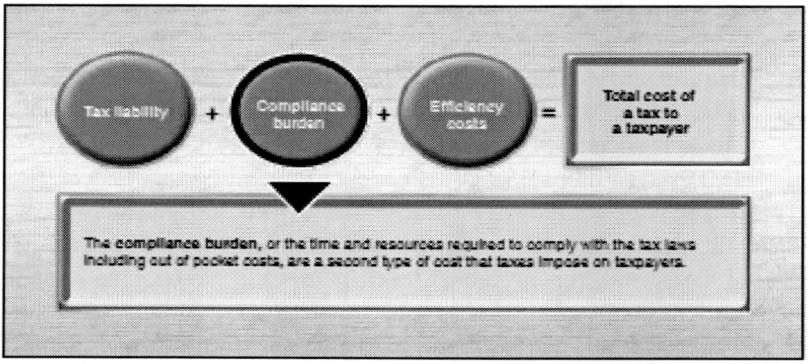


Source: GAO.

Figure 1. Compliance Burden Is One Cost Taxpayers Face in Complying with the Tax System.

The tax system also results in economic efficiency costs, which are reductions in economic well-being caused by changes in behavior due to taxes, government benefits, monopolies, and other forces that interfere in the market. Efficiency costs can take the form of lost output or consumption opportunities. For example, economists generally agree that the favorable tax treatment of owner-occupied housing distorts investment in the economy, resulting in too much investment in housing and too little business investment. Estimating efficiency costs associated with the tax system is challenging because it has extensive and diverse effects on behavior. In fact, in a 2005 report, we found no comprehensive estimates of the efficiency costs of the current federal tax system.[11] The two most comprehensive studies we found suggest that these costs are large—on the order of magnitude of 2 to 5 percent of GDP each year (as of the mid-1990s). However, the actual efficiency costs of the current tax system may not fall within this range because of uncertainty surrounding taxpayers' behavioral responses, changes in the tax code and the economy since the mid-1990s, and the fact that the two studies did not cover the full scope of efficiency costs.

Tax software and the use of paid tax return preparers may mitigate the need for taxpayers to understand complexities of the tax code. In 2010, IRS processed about 137 million returns. As we have previously reported, about 90 percent of returns are prepared by individual taxpayers or paid preparers using professional or commercial software. Software companies and paid preparers often act as surrogate tax administrators in that they keep abreast of tax law changes. A participant at the 2007 Joint Forum on Tax Compliance stated that taxpayers receiving assistance in preparing their individual tax returns, either from paid preparers or tax preparation software, are somewhat insulated from tax code complexity.[12]

However, while many paid tax preparers help taxpayers by using their expertise to help ensure that complex laws are understood, others may introduce their own mistakes. For example, in a limited investigation in 2006, all 19 of the tax return preparers who prepared returns for our undercover investigators produced errors, some with substantial consequences.[13] IRS's review of 2001 tax returns also found that tax returns prepared by paid preparers contained a significant level of errors. IRS audits of returns prepared by a paid preparer showed a higher error rate—56 percent—than audits of returns prepared by the taxpayer—47 percent.

## COMPLEXITIES IN REPORTING INCOME CONTRIBUTE TO THE TAX GAP BY PROVIDING OPPORTUNITIES FOR TAXPAYERS TO MISREPORT

Income measurement is straightforward for a large proportion of the individual taxpayer population: those who earn only labor and interest income and capital income within a retirement account generally have their income reported to them (and to the IRS) by the source of the income. However, substantial numbers of taxpayers who receive income from capital gains, rents, self-employment, and other sources often deal with complex tax laws, complicated calculations, and detailed record keeping. While complexities lead some taxpayers to make mistakes when reporting their income, some misreporting is due to intentional acts of tax evasion.

For example, IRS studies show that the majority of capital asset transactions and capital gains and losses were for securities transactions such as sales of corporate stock, mutual funds, bonds, options, and capital gain distributions from mutual funds. Taxpayers are required to report securities transactions on their federal income tax returns. To accurately report securities sales, the taxpayer must have records of the dates they acquired and sold the asset; sales price, or gross proceeds from the sale; cost or other basis of the sold asset; and resulting gains or losses.[14] They must report this information separately for short-term transactions and long-term transactions. Further, before taxpayers can determine any gains or losses from securities sales, they must determine if and how the original cost basis of the securities must be adjusted to reflect certain events, such as stock splits, nontaxable dividends, or nondividend distributions. Complex income-reporting requirements for securities transactions may contribute to taxpayers' misreporting their income. In 2006, we estimated that 8.4 million of the estimated 21.9 million taxpayers with securities transactions misreported their gains or losses for tax year 2001.[15] A greater estimated percentage of taxpayers misreported gains or losses from securities sales (36 percent) than capital gain distributions from mutual funds (13 percent), and most of the misreported securities transactions exceeded $1,000 of capital gain or loss.[16] This may be because taxpayers must determine the taxable portion of securities sales' income whereas they need only add up their capital gain distributions. Furthermore, about half of these taxpayers who misreported failed to accurately report the securities' basis, sometimes because they did not know the basis or failed to adjust the basis appropriately. Although we were not able to estimate the capital gains tax gap for securities, we were able to determine the direction of the misreporting. For securities sales, an estimated 64 percent of taxpayers underreported their income from securities (i.e., they understated gains or overstated losses) compared to an estimated 33 percent of taxpayers who overreported income (i.e., they overstated gains or understated losses).[17] For both underreported and overreported income, some taxpayers misreported over $400,000 in gains or losses. Small businesses—which include sole proprietorships and S corporations, among other entities—are subject to multiple layers of filing, reporting, and deposit requirements. These requirements reflect IRS's administration of a variety of tax and other policies, including income, employment, and excise taxes, as well as pension and other employee benefit programs. In considering the number of requirements, it is important to note that the requirements reflect many decisions and compromises made by Congress and administrations to accomplish their policy goals, including those that may benefit small businesses and other taxpayers.

Sole proprietors face significant complexities in reporting income. This complexity may contribute to the estimated $68 billion of the tax gap caused by sole proprietors underreporting their net business income, which can stem either from understated receipts or overstated expenses. For example, sole proprietors report their business-related profit or loss on their individual income tax return, and they can use their losses to offset other categories of income on their returns in the year that they incur the loss. Identifying which of a sole proprietor's payments qualify as business expenses and the amount to be deducted can be complex. For example, two types of payments—costs of goods sold and capital improvements—must be distinguished from other types of payments because they are treated differently under tax rules.[18] Expenses that are used partly for business and personal purposes can be deducted only to the extent they are used for business.

Individual taxpayers who are shareholders in S corporations may also experience difficulty because of complexity in income measurement. An S corporation is a federal business type that provides tax benefits and limited liability protection to shareholders. S corporations are not generally taxed at the entity level: income, losses, and deduction items pass through to the individual shareholders' income tax returns, and the shareholders are taxed on any net income. S corporations are to provide their shareholders and IRS with information on the allocation of income, losses, and other items.

As we have previously reported, one source of complexity for S corporation shareholders may arise when calculating basis—their ownership share of the corporation—in order to claim losses and deductions to offset other earned income.[19] Shareholders generally can only claim losses and deductions up to the amount of basis the shareholder has in the S corporation's stock and debt.[20] While the S corporation is required to send shareholders some information that can be used to calculate basis, S corporations are not required to report any basis calculations to shareholders. IRS officials and S corporation stakeholder representatives told us that calculating and tracking basis was one of the biggest challenges in complying with S corporation rules. In 2009, we recommended that Congress require S corporations to calculate shareholder's stock and debt basis as completely as possible and report the calculation to shareholders and IRS.21 In an analysis of IRS's annual examinations of individual tax returns that closed for fiscal years 2006 through 2008, we found the amount of the misreported losses that exceeded basis limitations was over $10 million, or about $21,600 per taxpayer.

## TAX EXPENDITURES ADD COMPLEXITY AND CONTRIBUTE TO THE TAX GAP BY PROVIDING OPPORTUNITIES FOR TAXPAYERS TO MAKE MISTAKES OR EVADE TAXES

The growing number of tax expenditures is among the causes of tax code complexity. Between 1974 and 2010, tax expenditures reported by the Department of the Treasury more than doubled in overall number from 67 to 173. Tax expenditures are an important means the government uses to address a wide variety of social objectives, from supporting educational attainment, to providing low-income housing, to ensuring retirement income, and many others. However, tax expenditures add to tax code complexity in part because they require taxpayers to learn about, determine their eligibility for, and choose between tax expenditures that have similar purposes. Tax expenditures also complicate tax planning, as taxpayers must predict their own future circumstances as well as future tax rules to make the best choice among provisions.

Savings incentives within the tax code illustrate how tax expenditures add to complexity. While the tax code includes numerous types of savings incentives—including those for healthcare and higher education—my statement will focus on retirement savings as a key example. Taxpayers can choose between traditional Individual Retirement Arrangements (IRA) and Roth IRAs for retirement savings.[22] Although the tax rules for distributions diverge for traditional and Roth IRAs, taxpayers may not know that a 10 percent early withdrawal penalty, with some exceptions, applies to both IRA types. Taxpayers also get confused over which IRA early withdrawals are not subject to penalties, in part because the exceptions differ for employer pension plans.

Additionally, both types of IRAs have rules governing eligibility to contribute, and contributions to each are subject to an annual limit. However, taxpayers may not understand that the annual contribution limit applies across traditional IRAs and Roth IRAs in combination, which may lead them to overcontribute. With regard to record-keeping burden, taxpayers with traditional or Roth IRAs must track the total amount of contributions in a given year and reasons for distributions to accurately report this information on their tax returns.

Frequent changes to IRA rules (such as increasing contribution limits and allowing workers to tap IRA assets for certain nonretirement purposes without an early withdrawal penalty) have also made tax planning more difficult for taxpayers.

As we reported in 2008, IRS research and enforcement data show that—in the aggregate—many taxpayers misreported millions of dollars in traditional IRA contributions and distributions on their tax returns.[23] We reported that in tax year 2001 the following occurred:

- Of the taxpayers who made deductible traditional IRA contributions, an estimated 14.8 percent[24] (554,657 taxpayers)[25] did not accurately report the IRA deduction on their individual tax returns—10.4 percent overstated their deductible contributions (that is, exceeded the applicable limit) and 4.4 percent underreported their deductible contributions (that is, reported less on their returns than they actually could deduct).[26] The understated net income due to these misreported traditional IRA contribution deductions was $392 million,[27] including both taxpayers who either overstated or understated their contribution deductions to a traditional IRA.

- Of the taxpayers who had taxable traditional IRA distributions, an estimated 14.6 percent[28] (1.5 million taxpayers)[29] misreported withdrawals from their traditional IRA distributions—13.7 percent understated (that is, reported an amount less than what the taxpayer withdrew) and 0.9 percent overstated IRA distributions (that is, reported an amount greater than what the taxpayer withdrew).[30] The underreported net income due to misreported IRA distributions was $6.3 billion,[31] including taxpayers who failed to report early distributions and the associated tax.

Taxpayers also make costly mistakes when choosing higher-education tax incentives. In a 2008 testimony, we reported that among tax filers who appeared to be eligible for a tax credit or tuition deduction in tax year 2005, about 19 percent, representing about 412,000 returns, failed to claim any of them.[32] The amount by which these tax filers failed to reduce their tax averaged $219; 10 percent of this group could have reduced their tax liability by over $500. In total, including both those who failed to claim a tax credit or tuition deduction and those who chose a credit or a deduction that did not maximize their benefit, we found that in 2005, 28 percent, or nearly 601,000 tax filers, did not maximize their potential tax benefit.

Some tax expenditures also provide taxpayers who intend to evade taxes with opportunities to do so. For example, the Treasury Inspector General for Tax Administration (TIGTA) reported in 2011 that the First-time Homebuyer Credit (FTHBC) and the subsequent changes made to the credit have confused taxpayers and allowed individuals to make fraudulent claims for the refundable credit.[33] For example, TIGTA reported many taxpayers claiming the credit appeared not to be first-time homebuyers because tax information indicated they had owned homes within 3 years prior to their new home purchase. The 2008 FTHBC provided taxpayers a refundable credit of up to $7,500 that must be repaid in $500 increments each year over 15 years beginning in the 2011 filing season.[34] According to recent IRS data, the total amount to be repaid by taxpayers is $7 billion. The American Recovery and Reinvestment Act of 2009 increased the maximum FTHBC credit to $8,000, with no payback required unless the home ceases to be the taxpayer's principal residence within 3 years. In 2009, we testified that IRS faced significant challenges in determining if taxpayers were complying with the numerous conditions for the credit.[35] For example, to determine eligibility, IRS had to verify that taxpayers had not owned a house in the previous 3 years and verify the closing date on home purchases. Other challenges included enforcing the $500 per year payback provision in the 2008 credit.

## STRATEGIES TO REDUCE THE TAX GAP PRESENT CHALLENGES AND TRADEOFFS

Multiple approaches are needed to reduce the tax gap. No single approach is likely to fully and cost-effectively address noncompliance since the noncompliance has multiple causes and spans different types of taxes and taxpayers. While the tax gap will remain a challenge into the future, the following strategies could help. These strategies could require actions by Congress or IRS.

### Enhancing Information Reporting

Enhancing information reporting can reduce complexity for taxpayers. It can also reduce the opportunities available for taxpayers to evade taxes by, for example, underreporting business income or filing fraudulent claims for tax credits. Generally, new requirements on third parties to submit information returns would require statutory changes, whereas improvements to existing information-reporting forms may be done administratively by IRS.

The extent to which individual taxpayers accurately report the income they earn has been shown to be related to the extent to which the income is reported to them and IRS by third parties or taxes on the income are withheld. For example, employers report most wages, salaries, and tip compensation to employees and IRS through Form W-2. Also, banks and other financial institutions provide information returns (Forms 1099) to account holders and IRS showing the taxpayers' annual income from some types of investments. Findings from IRS's study of individual tax compliance indicate that nearly 99 percent of these types of income are accurately reported on individual tax returns. For types of income for which there is little or no information reporting, individual taxpayers tend to misreport over half of their income.

One area where improved information reporting could help is higher-education expenses. Eligible educational institutions are required to report information on qualified tuition and related expenses for higher education to both taxpayers and IRS so that taxpayers can determine the amount of educational tax benefits that can be claimed.[36] However, the information currently reported by educational institutions on tuition statements sent to IRS and taxpayers (on Form 1098-T) may be confusing for taxpayers who use the form to prepare their tax returns and not very useful to IRS. IRS requires institutions to report on Form 1098-T either the (1) amount of payments received, or (2) amount billed for qualified expenses. IRS officials stated that most institutions report the amount billed and do not report payments. However, the amount billed may not equal the amount that can be claimed as a credit.[37] In order to reduce taxpayer confusion and enhance compliance with the eligibility requirements for higher-education benefits, in 2009 we recommended that IRS revise Form 1098-T to improve the usefulness of information on qualifying education expenses.[38]

Another area where improved information reporting could improve compliance is rental income. In 2008, we estimated that at least 53 percent of individual taxpayers with rental real estate misreported their rental real estate activities for tax year 2001, resulting in an estimated $12.4 billion of net misreported income.[39] IRS enforcement officials cited limited information reporting as a major challenge in ensuring compliance because without third-party information reporting, it is difficult for IRS to systematically detect taxpayers who fail to report any rent or determine whether the rent and expense amounts taxpayers report are accurate. In 2008, we recommended that IRS require third parties to report mortgaged property addresses to help IRS identify who may have misreported their rental real estate activity, but IRS did not adopt our recommendation because of third-party burden and a lack of an IRS compliance program to use such information. We made a similar recommendation in a 2009 report, which IRS is still evaluating as of December 2010.[40]

While information reporting reduces the complexity of reporting income for individual taxpayers, this tool can create costs for the third parties responsible for reporting the income to the taxpayer and IRS. For example, we previously reported that expanding information reporting on securities sales to include basic information would involve challenges for brokers and the IRS.[41] In particular, brokers would bear costs and burdens—even as taxpayers' costs and burdens decrease somewhat—and many issues would arise about how to calculate adjusted basis, which securities would be covered, and how information would be transferred among brokers.

In some cases it is difficult to identify third parties for whom a reporting requirement could be enforced without an undue burden on both the third parties and IRS. In a 2009 report, we found that a major reason why little information reporting on sole proprietor expenses exists is because of the difficulty identifying third parties.[42] For example, there is no third party who could verify the business use of cars or trucks by sole proprietors.

## Ensuring High-Quality Services to Taxpayers

Ensuring high-quality services is a necessary foundation for voluntary compliance, so action by IRS to improve the quality of services provided to taxpayers would be beneficial. High-quality services can help taxpayers who wish to comply but do not understand their obligations. IRS taxpayer services include education and outreach programs, simplifying the tax process, and revising forms and publications to make them electronically accessible and more easily understood by diverse taxpayer communities. For example, if tax forms and instructions are unclear, taxpayers may be confused and make unintentional errors. Ensuring high-quality taxpayer services would also be a key consideration in implementing any of the approaches for tax gap reduction. For example, expanding enforcement efforts would increase interactions with taxpayers, requiring processes to efficiently communicate with taxpayers. Changing tax laws and regulations would also require educating taxpayers about the new requirements in a clear, timely, and accessible manner.

For example, we previously reported that while taxpayers' access to telephone assistance in tax year 2009 was better than the previous year, it remained lower than in 2007, in part because of calls about tax law changes.[43] Despite heavy call volume, the accuracy of IRS responses to taxpayers' questions remained above 90 percent.

## Simplifying the Tax Code or Fundamental Tax Reform

Congressional efforts to simplify the tax code and otherwise alter current tax policies may help reduce the tax gap by making it easier for individuals and businesses to understand and voluntarily comply with their tax obligations. One way to simplify the tax code is to eliminate or combine tax expenditures, thereby helping reduce taxpayers' unintentional errors and limiting opportunities for tax evasion. As we have previously testified, the Government Performance and Results Act (GPRA) Modernization Act of 2010 (GPRAMA)[44] could help inform reexamination or restructuring efforts and lead to more efficient and economical executive-branch service delivery in overlapping program areas. The act is intended to identify the various agencies and federal activities—including spending programs, regulations, and tax expenditures—that contribute to crosscutting outcomes.[45]

While simplification can have benefits, it can also have drawbacks. Eliminating tax expenditures would reduce the incentives for the activities that were encouraged. Also, in 2005, we stated that changes to the tax system can create winners and losers.[46] The government may attempt to mitigate large gains and losses by implementing transition rules. Deciding if transition relief is necessary involves how to trade off between equity, efficiency, simplicity, transparency, and administrability.

Similar trade-offs exist with possible fundamental tax reforms that would move away from an income tax system to some other system, such as a consumption tax, national sales tax, or value-added tax. Fundamental tax reform would most likely result in a smaller tax gap if the new system has few tax preferences or complex tax code provisions and if taxable transactions are transparent. However, these characteristics are difficult to achieve in any system and experience suggests that simply adopting a fundamentally different tax system, whatever the economic merits, may not by itself eliminate any tax gap. For example, in 2008, we reported that some available data indicate a value-added tax may be less expensive to administer than an income tax. However, we found that like other systems, even a simple value-added tax—one that exempts few goods or services— has compliance risks and, largely as a consequence, generates administrative costs and compliance burden.[47] Similar to other taxes, adding complexity through exemptions or reduced rates for some goods or services generally decreases revenue and increases compliance risks because of the incentive to misclassify purchases and sales. Such complexity also increases the record-keeping burden on businesses and increases the government resources devoted to enforcement.

Any tax system could be subject to noncompliance, and its design and operation, including the types of tools made available to tax administrators, will affect the size of any corresponding tax gap. Further, the motivating forces behind tax reform include factors beyond tax compliance, such as economic effectiveness, equity, and burden, which could in some cases carry greater weight in designing an alternative tax system than ensuring the highest levels of compliance.

Policymakers may find it useful to compare any proposed changes to the tax code based on a set of widely accepted criteria for assessing alternative tax proposals. These criteria include the equity, or fairness, of the tax system; the economic efficiency, or neutrality, of the system; and the simplicity, transparency, and administrability of the system. These criteria can sometimes conflict, and the weight one places on each criterion will vary among individuals. Our publication, *Understanding the Tax Reform Debate: Background, Criteria, and Questions*, may be useful in guiding policymakers as they consider tax reform proposals.[48]

## Devoting Additional Resources to Enforcement

Devoting additional resources to enforcement has the potential to help reduce the tax gap by billions of dollars. However, determining the appropriate level of enforcement resources to provide IRS requires taking into account factors such as how effectively and efficiently IRS is currently using its resources, how to strike the proper balance between IRS's taxpayer service and enforcement activities, and competing federal funding priorities. If Congress were to provide IRS more enforcement resources, the amount that the tax gap could be reduced depends in part on factors such as the size of budget increases, how IRS manages any additional resources, and the indirect increase in taxpayers' voluntary compliance resulting from expanded enforcement. Providing IRS with additional funding would enable it to contact millions of potentially noncompliant taxpayers it currently identifies but cannot contact given resource constraints.

However, devoting additional resources to enforcement will not completely close the tax gap. For example, in a 2009 report, we reported that IRS's compliance programs focused on sole proprietors' underreporting of income addressed only a small portion of sole proprietor expense noncompliance.[49] Despite investing nearly a quarter of all revenue agent time in 2008, IRS was able to examine (audit) about 1 percent of estimated noncompliant sole proprietors. These exams are costly and yielded less revenue than exams of other categories of taxpayers, in part because most sole proprietorships are small in terms of receipts.

## Expanding Compliance Checks Before IRS Issues Refunds

IRS could reduce the tax gap by expanding compliance checks before issuing refunds to taxpayers. In April 2011, the Commissioner of Internal Revenue talked about a long-term vision to increase compliance activities before refunds are sent to taxpayers. In one example, IRS is exploring a requirement that third parties send information returns to IRS and taxpayers at the same time as opposed to the current requirement that some information returns go to taxpayers before going to IRS. The intent is to move to matching those information returns to tax returns during tax return processing. IRS currently matches data provided on over 2 billion information returns to tax returns only after the normal filing season. Matching during the filing season would allow IRS to detect and correct errors before it sends taxpayers their refunds, thereby avoiding the costs of trying to recover funds from taxpayers later.[50] This approach could also allow IRS to use its enforcement resources on other significant compliance problems. However, the Commissioner made clear that his vision for more prerefund compliance checks will take considerable time to implement. One prerequisite would be a major reworking of some fundamental IRS computer systems. To the extent that implementing this vision would require additional budgetary resources or changes in tax policies, Congress would play a key role.

## Using Consistent Definitions

If Congress changed the law to include more consistent definitions across tax provisions, then taxpayers could more easily understand and comply with their obligations. Higher-education tax preferences provide an example of inconsistent definitions for qualified education expenses. What tax filers are allowed to claim as a qualified higher-education expense varies between some of the various savings and credit provisions in the tax code. For example, while Coverdell education savings accounts and qualified tuition programs under section 529 of the Internal Revenue Code permit tax filers to include room and board as qualified expenses if the student is enrolled at least half time, the American Opportunity Credit and the Lifetime Learning Credit do not. These dissimilar definitions require that tax filers keep track of expenses separately, applying some expenses to some tax preferences, but not others.

There are no easy solutions to the tax gap, but addressing the tax gap is as important as ever before in the face of the nation's fiscal challenges.

Innovative thinking and the combined efforts of IRS and Congress will be needed now and in the years to come.

Chairman Baucus, Ranking Member Hatch, and Members of the Committee, this completes my prepared statement. I would be happy to respond to any questions you may have at this time.

## End Notes

[1] Tax expenditures are preferential provisions in the tax code, such as exemptions and exclusions of income from taxation, deductions, credits, deferral of tax liability, and preferential tax rates. Deciding whether an individual provision should be characterized as a tax expenditure is a matter of judgment, and disagreements about classification stem from different views about what should be included in the income tax base. As a practical matter, the term tax expenditure has been used in the federal budget for over three decades, and the tax expenditure concept—while not precisely defined—is a valid representation of one tool that the federal government uses to allocate resources. The home mortgage interest deduction and the Earned Income Tax Credit are examples of tax expenditures.

[2] GAO, Government Performance and Accountability: Tax Expenditures Represent a Substantial Federal Commitment and Need to Be Reexamined, GAO-05-690 (Washington, D.C.: Sept. 23, 2005).

[3] Throughout this statement, references to the tax gap refer to the gross tax gap unless otherwise noted.

[4] Taxpayers who receive filing extensions, pay their full tax liability by payment due dates, and file returns prior to extension deadlines are considered to have filed on time.

[5] For a summary of key outstanding recommendations, see GAO, Opportunities to Reduce Potential Duplication in Government Programs, Save Tax Dollars, and Enhance Revenue, GAO-11-318SP (Washington, D.C.: Mar. 1, 2011).

[6] For a more detailed discussion about data sources and methodologies used in estimating the tax gap, see GAO, Tax Compliance: Better Compliance Data and Long-term Goals Would Support a More Strategic IRS Approach to Reducing the Tax Gap, GAO-05-753 (Washington, D.C.: July 18, 2005).

[7] An information return is a tax document businesses and some individuals are required to file to report certain business transactions to the IRS. The requirement to file information returns is mandated by the IRS and associated regulations.

[8] Sums of tax expenditure estimates are useful for gauging the magnitude of tax spending, but need to be interpreted carefully because they do not take into account possible interactions between the individual tax code provisions. These estimates are based on data from the President's Fiscal Year 2012 Budget Request's list of tax expenditures, which is based upon current tax law enacted as of September 30, 2010. On December 17, 2010, the Tax Relief, Unemployment Insurance Reauthorization, and Job Creation Act of 2010 not only extended many tax expenditure provisions, but also extended income tax rates for the years 2011-12, thus affecting the estimates of many tax expenditures.

[9] As of May 2011, this recommendation has not been implemented.

[10] GAO, Tax Policy: Summary of Estimates of the Costs of the Federal Tax System, GAO-05-878 (Washington, D.C.: Aug. 26, 2005).

[11] GAO-05-878.

[12] GAO, Highlights of the Joint Forum on Tax Compliance: Options for Improvement and Their Budgetary Potential, GAO-08-703SP (Washington, D.C.: June 2008). GAO, the Congressional Budget Office, and the Joint Committee on Taxation convened the Joint Forum on Tax Compliance.

[13] GAO, Paid Tax Return Preparers: In a Limited Study, Chain Preparers Made Serious Errors, GAO-06-563T (Washington, D.C.: Apr. 4, 2006). Our findings cannot be generalized to the entire retail tax preparation community.

[14] Basis is generally the amount of a taxpayer's investment in a property for tax purposes.

[15] GAO, Capital Gains Tax Gap: Requiring Brokers to Report Securities Cost Basis Would Improve Compliance if Related Challenges Are Addressed, GAO-06-603 (Washington, D.C.: June 13, 2006). We are 95 percent confident that from 7.3 million to 9.5 million taxpayers misreported securities transactions and from 20.3 million to 23.5 million taxpayers had securities transactions.

[16] Percentage estimates have sampling errors of (+/-) 7 percent or less.

[17] Figures do not sum to 100 percent because some taxpayers misreported securities sales in a way that had no effect on the amount of income from the sales, for example in cases where taxpayers only misreported the securities' holding periods. Estimates have sampling errors of (+/-) 9 percent or less.

[18] To identify the cost of goods sold, businesses that manufacture or resell merchandise must follow tax rules that require valuing their inventory at the beginning and end of the tax year. Payments for capital improvements, such as start-up costs, business assets, and improvements, usually are not fully deducted in the current tax year but instead must be depreciated over a multiyear period.

[19] GAO, Tax Gap: Actions Needed to Address Noncompliance with S Corporation Tax Rules, GAO-10-195 (Washington, D.C.: Dec. 15, 2009).

[20] Stock basis begins with the shareholder's initial capital contribution to the S corporation or the initial cost of the stock purchased. That amount may increase or decrease each year. An income item will increase stock basis; a loss, deduction, or nondividend distribution will decrease stock basis, based on certain ordering rules. For losses and deductions that exceed a shareholder's stock basis, the shareholder is allowed to deduct the excess up to the shareholder's debt basis, which is created by loans that the shareholder personally made to the S corporation.

[21] As of December 2010, no action has been taken.

[22] The traditional IRA allows tax deferral on investment earnings until retirement distribution with an up-front tax deduction from taxable income for contributions by eligible taxpayers, and retirement distributions are taxable. In contrast, the Roth IRA allows nondeductible, after-tax contributions for eligible taxpayers, and retirement distributions, including investment earnings, are generally tax-free.

[23] GAO, Individual Retirement Accounts: Additional IRS Actions Could Help Taxpayers Facing Challenges in Complying with Key Tax Rules, GAO-08-654 (Washington, D.C.: Aug. 14, 2008).

[24] We are 95 percent confident that from 11.8 percent to 17.8 percent did not accurately report their traditional IRA deductions.

[25] Estimate has a margin of error of less than or equal to (+/-) 124,057.

[26] We are 95 percent confident that from 7.9 percent to 13.3 percent overstated their traditional IRA deductions. We are 95 percent confident that from 2.8 percent to 6.5 percent understated their traditional IRA deductions.

[27] Estimate has a margin of error of less than or equal to (+/-) $192 million.

[28] We are 95 percent confident that from 12.7 percent to 16.6 percent did not accurately report their traditional IRA distributions.

[29] Estimate has a margin of error of less than or equal to (+/-) 220,026.

[30] We are 95 percent confident that from 11.8 percent to 15.7 percent underreported their traditional IRA distributions. We are 95 percent confident that from 0.5 percent to 1.4 percent overreported their traditional IRA distributions.

[31] Estimate has a margin of error of less than or equal to (+/-) $2.2 billion.

[32] GAO, Higher Education: Multiple Higher Education Tax Incentives Create Opportunities for Taxpayers to Make Costly Mistakes, GAO-08-717T (Washington, D.C.: May 1, 2008).

[33] Treasury Inspector General for Tax Administration, Recovery Act: Administration of the First-Time Homebuyer Credit Indicates a Need for Improved Controls Over Refundable Credits, 2011-41-035 (Washington, D.C.: Mar. 31, 2011).

[34] The FTHBC is a refundable tax credit, meaning that it is paid out even if there is no tax liability or the credit exceeds the amount of any tax due.

[35] GAO, First-Time Homebuyer Tax Credit: Taxpayers' Use of the Credit and Implementation and Compliance Challenges, GAO-10-166T (Washington, D.C.: Oct. 22, 2009).

[36] 26 U.S.C. § 6050S. Qualified expenses are tuition and fees a student must pay to be enrolled at or attend an eligible educational institution, and other course-related fees and expenses only if the fees and expenses must be paid to the institution as a condition of enrollment or attendance.

[37] Currently, educational institutions are required to report information on the form 1098-T for qualified tuition expenses as well as information on the institution itself and the student. These requirements include, for example, reporting name, address, and taxpayer identification number (TIN) of the institution; name, address, and TIN of the student; and amount of payments received or the amount billed for qualified expenses during the calendar year.

[38] GAO, 2009 Tax Filing Season: IRS Met Many 2009 Goals, but Telephone Access Remained Low, and Taxpayer Service and Enforcement Could Be Improved, GAO-10-225 (Washington, D.C.: Dec. 10, 2009). In December 2010, IRS agreed to consider the feasibility of using Form 1098-T information in conjunction with its examination program.

[39] GAO, Tax Gap: Actions That Could Improve Rental Real Estate Reporting Compliance, GAO-08-956 (Washington, D.C.: Aug. 28, 2008).

[40] We recommended that IRS require third parties to provide information on the address of a home securing a mortgage, among other items. GAO, Home Mortgage Interest Deduction: Despite Challenges Presented by Complex Tax Rules, IRS Could Enhance Enforcement and Guidance, GAO-09-769 (Washington, D.C.: July 29, 2009).

[41] GAO-06-603. We reported that, among other things, Congress may wish to consider requiring brokers to report to both taxpayers and IRS the adjusted basis of securities that taxpayers sell. Congress included a provision requiring brokers to report basis information to IRS and taxpayers in the Energy Improvement and Extension Act of 2008. The provision took effect on January 1, 2011, and the Joint Committee on Taxation estimated the provision is expected to raise $6.7 billion in revenue through 2018.

[42] GAO, Tax Gap: Sole Proprietor Loss Deductions Could Improve Compliance but Would Also Limit Some Legitimate Losses, GAO-09-815 (Washington, D.C.: Sept. 10, 2009).

[43] GAO-10-225.

[44] Pub. L. No. 111-352, 124 Stat. 3866 (Jan. 4, 2011). GPRAMA amends the Government Performance and Results Act of 1993, Pub. L. No. 103-62, 107 Stat. 285 (Aug. 3, 1993).

[45] GAO, Government Performance: GPRA Modernization Act Provides Opportunities to Help Address Fiscal, Performance, and Management Challenges, GAO-11-466T (Washington, D.C.: Mar. 16, 2011).

[46] GAO, Understanding the Tax Reform Debate: Background, Criteria, & Questions, GAO-05-1009SP (Washington, D.C.: September 2005).

[47] GAO, Value-Added Taxes: Lessons Learned from Other Countries on Compliance Risks, Administrative Costs, Compliance Burden, and Transition, GAO-08-566 (Washington, D.C.: Apr. 4, 2008). The value-added tax is a consumption tax that is widely used around the world. A value-added tax is levied on the difference between a business's sales and its purchases of goods and services. Typically, a business calculates the tax due on its sales, subtracts a credit for taxes paid on its purchases, and remits the difference to the government.

[48] GAO-05-1009SP

[49] GAO-09-815.

[50] GAO, Taxpayer Account Strategy: IRS Should Finish Defining Benefits and Improve Cost Estimates, GAO-11-168 (Washington, D.C.: Mar. 24, 2011).

In: Tax Gaps
Editor: Rondell Meinke
ISBN: 978-1-62417-452-0


*Chapter 6*

# UPDATE ON REDUCING THE FEDERAL TAX GAP AND IMPROVING VOLUNTARY COMPLIANCE*

*U.S. Department of the Treasury*

## I. INTRODUCTION

The Internal Revenue Service (IRS) collects 96 percent of the government's total receipts, approximately $2.7 trillion in FY 2008. The vast majority of those revenues come from taxpayers who voluntarily report and pay the taxes that they owe. The IRS has estimated the overall voluntary compliance rate to be approximately 84 percent.

Despite the voluntary compliance rate and vigorous enforcement by the IRS, a significant amount of revenue remains unreported and unpaid. In 2005, the IRS estimated this gross tax gap to be approximately $345 billion. After subtracting revenue obtained through enforcement actions and other late payments, the IRS estimated the net tax gap to be approximately $290 billion. These estimates, which remain the most recent estimates available, were conducted using data collected in tax year 2001 and before.

As a result of an increase in funding included in the IRS FY 2009 budget, the Department of the Treasury (Treasury) and the IRS have recently initiated

* This is an edited, reformatted and augmented version of a U.S. Department of the Treasury publication, dated July 8, 2009.

intensive efforts to update the estimate of the tax gap on an ongoing basis, which will permit more regular and effective assessments. Consistent with its commitment to long-term fiscal soundness, the Administration is committed to working closely with Congress to narrow the tax gap, which imposes an unfair burden on every American who pays taxes in full. Ongoing updates of the tax gap estimate starting in 2011 will form the basis for regularly assessing progress towards that goal.

Building on reports previously released, this report is intended to provide a comprehensive overview of efforts to close the tax gap. This report is also intended to serve as a baseline for further work and discussion. After briefly discussing the nature and scope of the tax gap, this report summarizes previous Treasury and IRS tax gap reports and identifies the areas of strategic priority detailed in those reports. This report then summarizes the achievements, ongoing efforts, and new initiatives for achieving progress in each of those areas of strategic priority, organized according to the components of the strategy to reduce the tax gap detailed in prior reports.

As this report will make clear, the IRS and Treasury, working with Congress, are pursuing a wide range of initiatives, including a series of legislative proposals included in the Administration's FY 2010 budget. The Administration recognizes the particular value of those efforts and initiatives that improve voluntary compliance by making the tax filing process easier and more taxpayer-friendly. While aggressive enforcement activity can also help to narrow the tax gap, it is important to recognize that increased enforcement efforts require certain trade-offs. The Administration is committed to working closely with Congress to strike an appropriate balance to maximize revenue collection without imposing unreasonable compliance and enforcement burdens on the vast majority of individuals and businesses that fully and willingly pay what they owe.

## II. THE TAX GAP

The Tax Gap Map that follows illustrates the nature and scope of the tax gap based on data from 2001 and prior years. As this map shows, noncompliance takes three forms:

- Underreporting (not reporting one's full tax liability on a timely-filed return);

- Underpayment (not timely paying the full amount of tax reported on a timely-filed return); and
- Nonfiling (not filing required returns on time and not paying the full amount of tax that should have been shown on the required return).

The IRS has separate tax gap estimates for each of these three types of noncompliance. Underreporting (in the form of unreported receipts and overstated expenses) constitutes over 82 percent of the gross tax gap. The single largest sub-component of underreporting involves the individual income tax, which represents more than 50 percent of the total tax gap. Underpayment constitutes nearly 10 percent, and nonfiling almost 8 percent of the gross tax gap.

## III. PRIOR TAX GAP REPORTS

In September 2006, Treasury's Office of Tax Policy issued a Comprehensive Strategy for Reducing the Tax Gap.[1] The 2006 report provided a primer on the components and measures of the tax gap and a seven-component strategy for reducing the tax gap. The components of that strategy are:

1. Reduce Opportunities for Evasion
2. Make a Multi-Year Commitment to Research
3. Continue Improvements in Information Technology
4. Improve Compliance Activities
5. Enhance Taxpayer Service
6. Reform and Simplify the Tax Law
7. Coordinate with Partners and Stakeholders

Following on this report, the Internal Revenue Service in August 2007 issued a more detailed report on Reducing the Federal Tax Gap: A Report on Improving Voluntary Compliance.[2] Emphasizing the same seven components outlined above, the 2007 report outlined specific projects and initiatives, legislative proposals, and other actions designed to attack the sources of noncompliance in each area. Four key principles guided the development of the strategy and continue to guide Treasury and IRS efforts to improve compliance:

# TAX GAP MAP for Tax Year 2001 (in $ Billions)

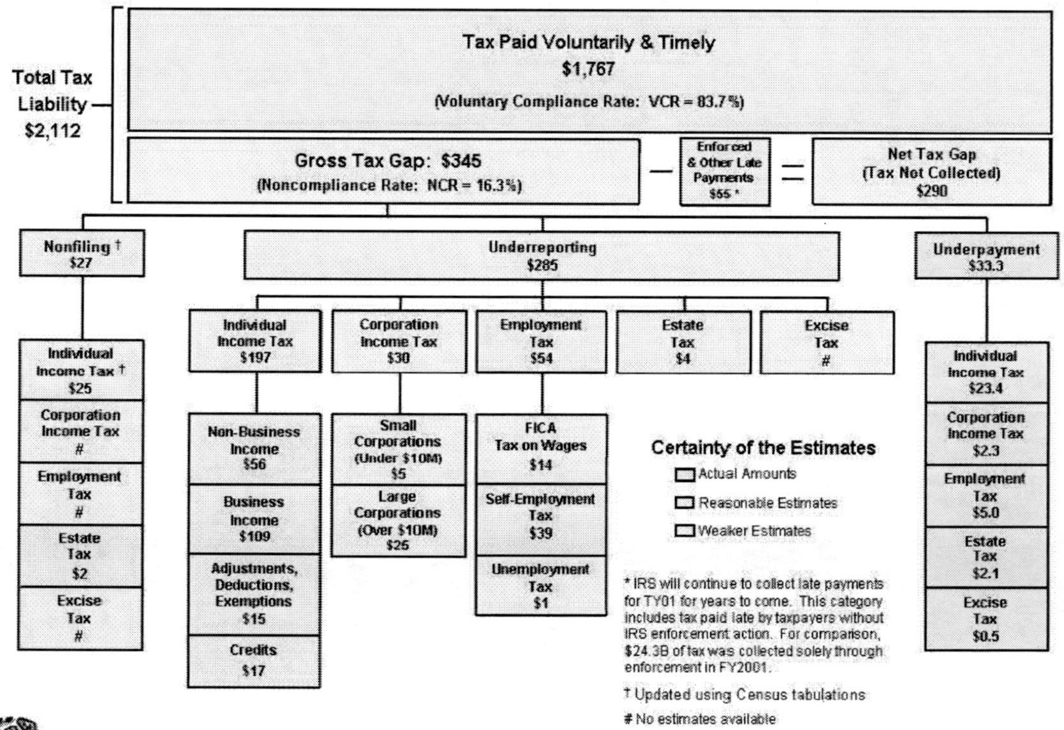


IRS • Research, Analysis, and Statistics

- First, both unintentional taxpayer errors and intentional taxpayer evasion should be addressed.
- Second, sources of noncompliance should be targeted with specificity.
- Third, enforcement activities should be combined with a commitment to taxpayer service.
- Fourth, policy positions and compliance proposals should be sensitive to taxpayer rights and maintain an appropriate balance between enforcement activity and imposition of taxpayer burden.

The 2007 tax gap report also provided a detailed explanation of the composition of the tax gap. That explanation is reproduced in full in the appendix of this report.

# IV. UPDATE ON EFFORTS TO REDUCE THE FEDERAL TAX GAP: PROGRESS ON STRATEGIC COMPONENTS

The prior tax gap reports detailed a seven-component strategy to reduce the tax gap and discussed and proposed specific actions to be taken within each component. This section of the report provides an update on those efforts, including a discussion of new proposals. The following section discusses the current IRS Strategic Plan, issued subsequent to the 2007 tax gap report, which covers FY 2009-2013, and outlines five long-term measures for evaluating the IRS' progress in achieving its goals, which directly relate to the tax gap strategy.

## Component 1. Reduce Opportunities for Evasion

### *Implement and Expand Information Reporting Authorities*

Previous reports have outlined the relationship between voluntary compliance and the degree to which income tax return items are "visible" to the IRS. Reporting compliance is highest where parties other than the taxpayer are required to file information reports and withhold taxes from payments made. From the taxpayer's perspective, information reporting can lead to significant administrative simplification.

Most Americans receive W-2 forms at the end of each year, which reduces the taxpayer's burden by eliminating the need to gather records or perform computations. W-2 recipients with no other major source of income can simply transcribe information from the W-2 form directly onto the tax return. For those taxpayers who e-file, the process is simplified even further, as the data from the W-2 can be electronically imported. At the same time, W-2 forms facilitate the ability of the IRS to detect non-compliance. To improve compliance and minimize error, Treasury and IRS have been focused on implementing several new information reporting regimes recently authorized by Congress.

- *Credit and debit card payments to businesses.* Starting in January 2011, organizations that process credit and debit card payments for merchants must annually report the amount of these payments to the recipient businesses and to the IRS. Treasury and IRS are actively working on the implementing regulations and soliciting input and feedback from taxpayers, banks, and credit card processors.
- *Cost basis reporting.* Starting in January 2011, brokerage firms must annually report cost basis and holding period information to customers and to the IRS in addition to gross proceeds from securities transactions. These information reports will make it easier for taxpayers to compute the net amount of gain or loss and will have a significant effect on reducing misreported capital gains.

In addition, the Administration's budget for FY 2010 includes the following significant new information reporting proposals:

- *Payments to Corporations.* The FY 2010 budget proposals would require businesses to file information returns for payments to a corporation for any services (such as accounting services or consultancy services) or certain gains aggregating to $600 or more per year.
  This would end current practice under a longstanding regulatory regime that exempts certain payments to corporations from general requirements for information reporting. These information reports will serve as reminders to the corporate recipients to include these amounts in gross receipts and will make these amounts visible to the IRS for targeted compliance programs.
- *Rental Property Expense Payments.* The FY 2010 budget proposals would require taxpayers who receive rental income and deduct expenses on rental activities to file information returns for rental property expense payments to any service provider or contractor that

performs work on rental properties. This would make the reporting requirements for taxpayers engaged in rental real estate activities consistent with the requirements for other business taxpayers.

- *Certain Government Payments for Property and Services.* Some government vendors fail to meet their tax filing and payment obligations, and compliance would likely increase significantly if those payments were automatically reported by the governmental entity making the payment.
  The FY 2010 budget proposals would therefore require Federal, state, and local governments to report information on non-wage payments made for the procurement of property or services. Exceptions are anticipated for certain categories of payments and recipients.
- *Private Separate Accounts of Life Insurance Companies.* The proposals would require life insurance companies to report account information for any contracts invested in a private separate account. The reporting of this information would help the IRS determine whether earnings on investments in separate accounts are taxable income to the holder or are tax-free or tax-deferred.
- *Requiring Certified Taxpayer Identification Numbers (TINs) from Contractors.* Without accurate taxpayer identifying information, the effectiveness of information reporting requirements is limited. Therefore, the FY 2010 budget proposal would require contractors to provide TINs to the businesses from which they receive payments, and require those businesses to verify the TINs. If a contractor failed to furnish an accurate certified TIN, the business paying the contractor would be required to withhold.
- *Increased Penalties for Failure to Properly Report Information.* Penalties for failure to properly report information have not been increased since they were first established in 1989. Increasing those penalties will provide a stronger incentive for compliance with information reporting requirements.
  Accordingly, the FY 2010 budget proposal would increase by 100 percent the current per-return penalties for failure to file most information returns and would substantially increase the maximum penalties that can be assessed in a calendar year. In addition, the proposal calls for adjusting the penalty amounts for inflation every five years.

### *Additional Fiscal Year 2010 Budget Proposals*

In addition to the information reporting proposals outlined above, the Administration's FY 2010 budget proposes an expansive set of additional tools or requirements to reduce opportunities for evasion and other non-compliance.

### Improving compliance by businesses

- *E-filing by Certain Large Organizations.* Mandate electronic filing for all corporations and partnerships required to file Schedule M-3 (Net Income or Loss Reconciliation).
  Expand the current regulatory authority to require e-filing by other large organizations (such as certain large exempt organizations). This would provide tax return information in a more uniform electronic form, enhancing the ability of the IRS to focus more productively its audit activities.
- *Clarification of Liability for Federal Employment Taxes of Employee Leasing Companies and Their Clients.* Set forth standards for holding employee leasing companies jointly and severally liable with their clients for Federal employment taxes under certain circumstances. Providing standards for when an employee leasing company and its clients will be held liable for Federal employment taxes will facilitate the assessment, payment, and collection of those taxes.

### Strengthening Tax Administration

- *Assessment of Criminal Restitution as Tax.* Allow the IRS and Treasury to immediately assess, without issuing a statutory notice of deficiency, and collect as a tax debt court-ordered restitution in criminal tax cases. Since court-ordered restitution in criminal tax cases currently cannot be assessed as a tax, the IRS cannot use its existing assessment systems to collect and enforce the restitution obligations. This leads to unnecessary duplication of effort, delay, and confusion.
- *Offer-In-Compromise Application Rules.* Eliminate the current-law requirement that an initial offer-in-compromise include a nonrefundable payment of a portion of the taxpayer's offer. Eliminating this requirement would expand access to the offer-in-compromise program and thereby improve IRS' ability to collect the portion of a tax liability that the taxpayer can pay.
- *IRS Access to Information in the National Directory of New Hires (NDNH).* Expand IRS access to the NDNH for general tax

administration purposes, including data matching, verification of taxpayer claims during return processing, and preparation of substitute returns for non-compliant taxpayers.

Access to the NDNH would increase IRS productivity by reducing the amount of IRS resources dedicated to obtaining and processing data without reducing the current levels of taxpayer privacy.

- *Repeated Willful Failure to File a Tax Return.* Create an aggravated failure-to-file criminal penalty for any person who willfully fails to file tax returns in any three years of five consecutive years if the aggregated tax liability is at least $50,000. Such failure to file would be classified as a felony with a penalty of a fine of not more than $250,000 ($500,000 for a corporation) or imprisonment of not more than five years, or both. These increased criminal penalties would help deter multiple willful failure-to-file tax returns.
- *Tax Compliance with Local Jurisdictions.* Treat Indian Tribal Governments (ITGs) that impose alcohol, tobacco, or fuel excise or income or wage taxes as States for purposes of information sharing to the extent necessary for ITG tax administration. Treating ITGs as States for information sharing purposes would allow greater sharing of information between the Federal government and ITGs and thereby support Federal and ITG compliance activities.
- *Statute of Limitations where State Tax Adjustment Affects Federal Tax Liability.* Create an additional exception to the general three-year statute of limitations for assessment of Federal tax liability resulting from adjustments to State or local tax liability. The statute of limitations would be extended only for items related to the State tax adjustment.

  The proposal would remove the current statute of limitations as a barrier to the effective use by the IRS of state and local tax adjustment reports when the reports are provided by the state or local revenue agency to the IRS with little time remaining to make assessments at the Federal level.
- *Investigative Disclosure.* Clarify that the taxpayer privacy laws do not prohibit Treasury and IRS officers and employees from identifying themselves, their organization, and the nature and subject of an investigation when contacting third parties in connection with a civil or criminal tax investigation.

  This clarification would facilitate investigations by IRS officers and employees while setting forth clear guidance for taxpayers.

- *Electronic Filing by Tax Return Preparers.* Permit regulations to require electronic filing by tax return preparers who file more than 100 tax returns in a calendar year. Electronic filing benefits taxpayers and the IRS because it decreases processing errors, expedites processing and payment of tax refunds, and allows the IRS to efficiently maintain up-to-date taxpayer records.

**Expand Penalties**

- *Bad Check Penalty.* Clarify, expand, and update the bad check penalty to cover all commercially acceptable instruments of payment, including electronic checks and other payment forms. At present, only checks and money orders are covered by the bad check penalty.
- *Penalties for Failure to Comply with Electronic Filing Requirements.* Establish a penalty for failure to comply with electronic filing requirements of $25,000 for a corporation or $5,000 for a tax-exempt organization.

  This penalty would not supersede existing penalties for failure to file in any format. Although there are additions to tax for the failure to file returns under current law, there is no specific penalty in the Internal Revenue Code for failure to comply with a requirement to file electronically.

***Administration's Proposals and Efforts to Combat Under-Reporting of Offshore Income***

The President has made addressing under-reporting of income earned or held through offshore accounts or entities a top priority for his Administration. The Administration has developed a comprehensive approach to combating offshore tax evasion by U.S. taxpayers that includes legislative proposals, efforts to increase exchange of tax information with other countries, and increased enforcement.

## Legislative Proposals

The Administration's budget for FY 2010 provides various legislative proposals to address offshore tax evasion, including:

- Reforming the existing IRS "Qualified Intermediary" (QI) program to require additional information reporting from QIs so that the IRS will receive the same level of information on U.S. taxpayers from QI participants that it does from U.S. financial institutions.

- Requiring withholding of tax, in appropriate circumstances, on payments made through intermediaries that are not QIs. This measure would discourage U.S. and foreign persons from attempting to avoid U.S. tax by providing incorrect self-certification to intermediaries or otherwise relying on the lack of information reporting required from foreign intermediaries that are not QIs.
- Denying the benefits of reduced withholding tax rates to certain foreign entities unless the entities identify their owners. This measure would help ensure that persons that are not entitled to an exemption from withholding tax or a reduced rate of withholding tax do not arrange to receive payments through entities that appear to qualify for such an exemption or reduced rate.
- Requiring taxpayers and financial institutions to report to the IRS on cross-border transfers of certain assets.
- Allowing the IRS to make certain legal presumptions to minimize the effect of nondisclosure on IRS investigations and enforcement proceedings when U.S. taxpayers fail to fully disclose their offshore accounts.
- Extending the statute of limitations and imposing increased penalties when certain required information returns are not filed.

## Exchanging Tax Information with Other Countries

Access to information from other countries is critically important to combating offshore tax evasion. For this reason, the United States has been a leader in increasing information exchange in tax matters.

We have worked through the Organisation for Economic Co-operation and Development (OECD) to establish standards on transparency and exchange of information for tax purposes, and have strongly encouraged countries to adopt these standards.

The United States has been more active in broadening the scope of information that countries agree to exchange through tax treaties and in negotiating and implementing tax information exchange agreements (TIEAs).

The United States will continue to update existing tax treaties with insufficient exchange of information provisions.

Treasury recently concluded negotiation of updated tax treaty information exchange provisions with two key countries, Luxembourg and Switzerland, and will work toward swift ratification and implementation of those new agreements.

Treasury will also continue to enter into new TIEAs, such as the agreements that the United States recently signed with Liechtenstein and Gibraltar.

The United States also will begin expanding its focus with respect to exchange of tax information from advocating international adoption of OECD standards to assessing international implementation of the standards adopted. Consistent with recommendations made by the United States, the G-20 London Summit Declaration called on appropriate bodies to conduct and strengthen objective peer review processes.

Accordingly, Treasury will work to establish a robust peer review process to assess implementation of the OECD standards through an expanded version of the OECD-organized Global Forum on Transparency and Exchange of Tax Information, which currently includes OECD members and more than 40 other jurisdictions. Peer review should act to improve international implementation of tax information exchange and thereby help to ensure that such exchange helps to support U.S. taxation of income earned or held through offshore accounts or entities.

## Increasing Enforcement

Finally, the President's FY 2010 budget also includes strong support for international enforcement. With the FY 2010 initiative funding, the IRS would hire nearly 800 additional employees dedicated to addressing a broad range of international tax enforcement concerns.

The initiative will increase examinations of complex international structures, cross-border transactions, and offshore activity on both corporate and individual returns. The Administration's continued support of IRS enforcement is described in greater detail below.

### *Status Update*

The following chart provides a status update on the full range of initiatives underway to reduce opportunities for evasion. In addition to the new initiatives detailed above, this chart catalogues the progress of initiatives previously reported in the 2006 and 2007 tax gap reports.

| Action Items | Status |
|---|---|
| Work with Congress to enact legislative proposals included in the Administration's FY 2010 Budget | In process |
| Implement recently enacted tax gap legislative proposals | Cost basis and merchant card reporting implementation:<br>• Issued announcement in January 2009 enabling merchant card and third party settlement organizations to begin TIN validation<br>• Issued two notices in February 2009 requesting public comments on the two reporting requirements<br>• Developing new forms, business requirements, compliance programs, andIT solutions<br>• Preparing proposed regulations and draftforms for public comment in Summer 2009<br>• Participating in ongoing meetings with stakeholders to work through implementation issues<br><br>Other proposals already implemented:<br>• Revised collection due process for employment taxes<br>• Increased preparer penalties<br>• Implemented erroneous refund claim penalties |
| Develop regulations and other published guidance clarifying ambiguous areas of the law, targeting specific areas of noncompliance and preventing abusive behavior | Our goal is to release 85 percent of the items appearing on the 2008-2009 priority guidance plan by 9/30/09. Examples include rules in the following areas:<br>• International restructurings<br>• Repatriation of foreign earnings<br>• Transfer pricing and cost sharing<br>• Foreign tax credit generator transactions<br>• Intermediary tax shelters<br>• Withholding tax application to business income earned by foreign partners in US partnerships<br>• Application of the excise tax on reinsurance of US risks by foreign insurers not in business in the US<br>• Corporate "inversions"<br>• Preparer penalties<br>• Welfare benefit funds<br>• Transactions of interest that involve charitable remainder trusts and controlledforeign corporations<br>• By 8/30/09, will release the priority guidance plan for 2009-2010 |

## Component 2: Make a Multi-Year Commitment to Research

### *Measuring the Tax Gap*

In 2005, the IRS released preliminary results of a major research effort to quantify the tax gap using data from tax year 2001 and before. The IRS in following years arrived at the estimate of the gross tax gap of $345 billion for tax year 2001. An update of the tax gap estimate based on more recent data is needed, and the IRS is working on delivering such an estimate in 2011. Updated estimates will help the IRS measure progress against its existing long-term goal of an 86 percent voluntary compliance rate for Tax Year 2009.[3]

To ensure that the Administration and Congress alike have access to more useful, up-to-date estimates of the tax gap, the Treasury and the IRS have begun to implement a long-term strategy to move away from occasional, large-scale efforts to estimate the tax gap and instead update tax gap estimates on an ongoing basis. The IRS's FY 2009 budget included funding to improve tax gap estimates, better measure non-compliance, and improve detection of non-compliance.

As part of the effort to update the tax gap estimate, the IRS is currently completing a reporting compliance study on Subchapter S corporations for 2003 and 2004 tax years, and plans to release the results later this year. The IRS is also currently conducting research on reporting compliance with the individual income tax for tax years 2006 and 2007, and will soon begin looking at tax year 2008 tax returns (filed in 2009). The data for these three years will provide the necessary baseline for regular updates to the individual income tax gap, which can begin in calendar year 2011.

The IRS is also conducting a pilot project to extend studies of individual income tax returns to include a small sample of returns with international addresses. While the research is still in exploratory stages, if representative compliance data for this population can be extrapolated, this approach could allow us to better estimate one portion of the international tax gap.

Finally, the IRS is currently preparing to launch a study of employment tax reporting and filing compliance, with field work beginning in October 2009. This study will also be conducted over multiple tax years, with the goal of eventually providing regular estimates of employment tax compliance levels and the drivers of non-compliance.

In addition to developing more recent data on which to base an updated estimate of the tax gap, the IRS will also continue to explore ways to improve research methodologies to better measure non-compliance and to improve its ability to target the sources of non-compliance.

### *Status Update*

The following chart provides a status update on the research and measurement efforts currently underway or completed since the release of prior tax gap reports:

| Action Items | Status |
|---|---|
| Undertake additional compliance studies, including S Corporations and individuals | • Completed S Corporation exams (analysis ongoing)<br>• Conducted TY2006 National Research Program (NRP) Form 1040 exams (analysis ongoing)<br>• Conducting TY2007 NRP Form 1040 exams (ongoing)<br>• Provide ongoing updates to level of tax gap attributable to underpayment (as shown in the Tax Gap Map, this amount is an actual amount, not an estimate) |
| Update tax gap estimates using new and existing data | • In process, as described above |
| Research the effect of service on taxpayer compliance | • Engaging in three significant research projects linking IRS service to compliance (in process) |
| Research the relationship between complexity, burden, and compliance | • Preparing survey of individual taxpayers to improve burden estimates (in process)<br>• Engaging in three research projects focusing on relationships between complexity, burden, and compliance (in process) |

## Component 3: Continue Improvements in Information Technology

The IRS continues to focus on improving the technology infrastructure that supports its service and enforcement programs. Improved information technology capabilities will help make early detection and intervention efforts more effective, improve case selection, and allow the IRS to offer better, more user-friendly service to taxpayers.

### *Increasing E-File Rate*

Electronic filing is a critical component of the effort to improve voluntary compliance and close the tax gap. By simplifying the filing process for taxpayers, decreasing processing errors, and expediting the processing and payment of tax refunds, electronic filing makes the tax-filing process less onerous for taxpayers and allows the IRS to update taxpayer records more efficiently. Through sustained focus and outreach, the e-file rate has been steadily increasing for years. The 2008 e-file rate for individuals was 58 percent, up from 31 percent in 2001. Tax filing results thus far in 2009 already reflect a significant increase in this rate.

The Administration is committed to achieving an overall e-file rate of 80 percent. The IRS recent published *an in-depth research study* on ways to increase the e-file rate.[4] The study showed that approximately 85 percent of individual tax returns were filed by paid preparers, or by individuals via third-party software products. The study also showed that over 98 percent of paid preparer returns were completed using software, and yet a substantial number of tax returns are ultimately printed and mailed to the IRS. The Administration believes that in order to sustain progress toward the 80 percent goal, the Treasury should be authorized to require electronic filing from tax return preparers who file more than 100 tax returns in a calendar year. The President's FY 2010 budget includes the legislative proposal necessary to provide this authority. Additionally, the IRS has been working on a modernized electronic filing (MeF) platform that provides real-time processing of tax returns and improves error detection. This new platform will improve detection of errors during the initial filing process, rather than after the fact, and will therefore reduce the number of filing errors that contribute to the tax gap. MeF is currently processing electronically filed tax returns for corporations, partnerships, excise tax filers, and exempt organizations. The number of tax returns filed through the MeF system increased 49 percent in 2008 to more than 3 million accepted returns, and volumes are projected to reach 4 million accepted returns for 2009. Starting in 2010, the IRS plans to roll out Form 1040 and its family of related schedules on the MeF platform, which will extend the benefits of the MeF platform to individual taxpayers as well.

### *Core Taxpayer Account Database*

The IRS has made significant progress in updating its core taxpayer account database, the Customer Account Data Engine. Moving away from its legacy technology, the IRS has devoted resources towards a new, relational database structure, which will enhance the flexibility, responsiveness, and timeliness of the IRS' service and enforcement functions. Nearly 40 million taxpayer accounts were processed using this modernized taxpayer account database in 2009.

This new database is the most important element of the IRS' strategy for the next generation of taxpayer service and compliance applications that are needed to address the tax gap. The Administration's FY 2010 budget includes a program increase of $23 million to accelerate this important work.

### *Applying Enhanced Information Technology to Ongoing Operations*

The IRS continues to deliver significant enhancements to the systems that support its core operations.

For example, the Automated Underreporter (AUR) program, a mechanized system that helps to identify discrepancies in returns, sends notices to taxpayers when amounts reported on individual tax returns and amounts reported by third parties don't match. Improvements to the AUR program have enhanced workload selection and improved the overall productivity of the program.

AUR case closures have increased from 2.0 million in 2004 to 3.5 million in 2008. The expansion of the AUR program has allowed the IRS to increase coverage in key areas of non-compliance.

### *Status Update*

The following provides a status update on the full range of information technology initiatives underway or completed since the release of previous tax gap reports:

| Action Items | Status | |
|---|---|---|
| Use technology to improve high income and non-EITC exam workload selection and method of delivery and assess the effectiveness of the exam treatment stream on selected non-filer cases | • | Implemented new selection and classification criteria based on NRP results |
| | • | Implemented automated case screening and selection process |
| Expand Automated Underreporter (AUR) program to include additional income types | • | Expanded use of automatic notices |
| Evaluate the AUR matching process, and implement an improved case scoring and selection concept to select the most productive cases. | • | Reengineered AUR matching process to improve coverage, maximize resource utilization, and increase AUR closures |
| | • | Implemented improved workload selection tools |
| Expand the AUR Soft Notice Test, which involves asking taxpayers to voluntarily self-correct for future years | • | Developed system requirements Performed test for approximately 30,000 taxpayers in FY2009 and expect to perform follow-up test of 30,000 additional taxpayers in FY2010 |

**(Continued)**

| Action Items | Status |
|---|---|
| Develop enhancements to the Compliance Data Warehouse to improve workload identification and prioritization algorithms, allowing better evaluation of alternative treatment streams and ensuring Collection cases receive the most efficient and effective treatments | • Completed |
| Update the Collection inventory management system to improve functionality and navigation and provide capability to interface with other modernized systems | • Nationwide deployment in process |
| Automate lien delivery, recording, and release processes with state and local jurisdiction to improve the timeliness of lien filing, lien releases, and the payment of fees | • Not yet started (currently unfunded) |
| Test the use of statistical modeling techniques within TEGE to detect high-risk compliance patterns in order to use data to expand and improve examination selection | • In process |
| Develop and implement a set of compliance decision analytic tools that will support analysis of Tax Exempt and Government Entities (TE/GE) returns and other data to detect compliance trends and improve case and issue selection | • In process |
| Implement a new TE/GE electronic examination system (TREES) that will consolidate agent work papers to increase the accuracy and efficiency of the examination process | • Completed |
| Build and implement modernized e-file (MeF) receipt of electronic transmissions for additional tax forms | • Deployed Form 1120F replacement in January 2008 and Form 990 replacement in January 2009<br>• Developing first phase of the Form 1040 series for deployment in 2010 |

## Component 4: Improve Compliance Activities

### *Multi-Year Investment in IRS Enforcement*

The Administration's FY 2010 budget continues strong support of IRS enforcement, which will support a sustained focus in the areas of greatest risk. The budget request includes program increases of $332.2 million for investments in strong compliance programs, including a robust portfolio of international enforcement initiatives. The priorities include international enforcement, improving compliance programs dealing with businesses and high income individuals, expanding the use of document matching techniques to combat misreporting of income by business taxpayers, and improving collection operations, including the creation of two new Automated Collection System (ACS) sites.

The Administration's FY 2010 budget includes funding for an additional 15 tax specialists in Treasury's Office of Tax Policy. These new specialists will help to ensure that Treasury possesses capabilities sufficient to support rigorous analysis and implementation of revenue policy, including tax gap reduction.

The Administration's FY 2010 budget also outlines a multi-year investment to deal more effectively with the ever-increasing volume and complexity of international transactions. The initiative will add nearly 800 enforcement personnel to address the underreporting of tax associated with international transactions as well as domestic taxpayers involved with offshore activities.

The FY 2010 budget also contemplates a significant investment in enhancing and expanding the IRS' collection operation to address the tax gap attributable to underpayment of tax. From FY 2005 to FY 2008, the IRS achieved a 27.2 percent increase in collection efficiency, when over the same time period collection staffing decreased seven percent. The FY 2010 investment will allow the IRS to build on its efficiency gains, undertake pilot projects to further improve efficiency, and broaden overall collection coverage.

In total, the new enforcement personnel contemplated by the Administration's FY 2010 budget are estimated to generate $2.0 billion in additional annual enforcement revenue once the new hires reach full potential in FY 2012.

The IRS is constantly assessing the compliance landscape, and adapting and investing in its programs as needed to ensure an appropriate balance among its enforcement programs.

### *Status Update*

Expanding on the new priorities and initiatives discussed above, the following chart provides a status update on the enforcement initiatives currently underway or completed since the release of prior tax gap reports:

| Action Items | Status |
| --- | --- |
| Increase audit coverage and better target returns for examination | • Updated selection scores (DIF/Discriminate Information Function) based on NRP results<br>• Increased Schedule C audits |
| | • Updating selection criteria based on results of NRP (in process)<br>• Improving correspondence exam case selection methodologies (in process)<br>• Began significant compliance hiring initiative in FY09 |
| Enhance the ability to identify and address<br>tax schemes of business and individuals involving offshore activity, address illegitimate use of tax havens to shelter income, and increase information matching and examination activity for individuals living abroad | • Working with Congress to secure<br>requested FY 2010 funds for nearly 800 new international enforcement personnel. Funding request of $128M to increase international enforcement efforts.<br>• Engaging in voluntary disclosure initiative for taxpayers with undeclared offshore accounts<br>• Completed pilot phase of the Broker Compliance Initiative Project<br>• Developing additional compliance initiative projects in the areas of private banking and offshore merchant accounts<br>(in process)<br>• Issued regulations relating to transfer pricing, foreign tax credits, and foreign trusts (regulations relating to cross border restructuring in process)<br>• Implemented the Shelter Data Management System (SDM), and implementation of the larger Selection and Workload Classification system is in process<br>• Expanded the use of the OECD Abusive Transaction Database to identify emerging abusive transactions and issues |

| Action Items | Status |
|---|---|
| Enhance collection programs and increase | • Working with Financial Management |
| the Federal Payment Levy Program (FPLP) using third-party data | Service (FMS) and Centers for Medicare and Medicaid Services (CMS) to determine feasibility of adding Medicare payments |
| Work with other federal agencies regarding FPLP | • Expanded FPLP to include Defense Finance<br>• and Accounting Service salary payment files, Department of Defense Civilian Employees, HHS, EPA, and Department of Energy Entered into agreements with DoD to add additional Federal wage and other payments |
| Improve compliance by tax preparers | • Announced IRS review of tax return |
| through implementation of the Service-wide Enforcement Preparers Strategy | preparers (recommendations to be made by end of 2009) |
| Improve collection selection criteria and filters for balance due and non-filer cases, including identifying and addressing<br>potential high income non-filers | • Expanded the use of third-party information and research to enhance case selection<br>• Refining decision analytics and developing new model to enhance case selection (in process)<br>• Finalized Service-wide non-filer strategy |
| Litigate cases, work settlements, and design large scale resolution initiatives for tax shelter transactions to deter noncompliance | • Engaged in settlement initiatives including Son of Boss, LILO/SILO, Distressed Asset Trust (DAT), stock option transactions, and the overall Global Settlement Initiative<br>• Litigated and continued to litigate unresolved cases |
| Initiate a project using Combined Annual Wage Reporting (CAWR) data to identify tax-exempt organizations that may not be properly reporting and paying employment tax | • Analyzed results and documented lessons for future CAWR initiatives |
| Increase criminal enforcement on abusive schemes, corporate fraud, employment tax, egregious non-filers, and Bank Secrecy Act violations | • Achieved average conviction rate over 90 percent for the combined component programs and publicity rates over 80 percent |
| Improve the alignment and allocation of Service-wide resources to identify, develop, and resolve challenges better in the global taxation arena | • Moved forward with significant international<br>• compliance initiatives (in process)<br>• Used International Planning and Operations<br>• Council to identify opportunities to conduct |

**(Continued)**

| Action Items | Status |
|---|---|
| | • cross-divisional exams and enhance cross-divisional identification and referral of emerging international compliance issues<br>Realigned international resources to improve integration and leverage expertise<br>Increased international examiner hiring (ongoing)<br>Developing processes to evaluate referrals and identify and assess international and U.S. possessions compliance issues |
| Improve tax administration to deal more effectively with increased emphasis on globalization by all corporate and individual taxpayers | • Moved forward with significant international compliance initiatives (in process)<br>• Expanded information sharing through increased membership and broader focus in the Joint International Tax Shelter<br>• Information Centre (JITSIC) by adding Japan, adding a London office, and adding<br>• China and Korea as observers<br>• Introduced new Form M-3 for Form 1120F to gather information on foreign corporations<br>Revised Form 5471 for international transactions (in process)<br>Providing education and guidance to withholding agents of their responsibilities to withhold on Fixed, Determinable, Annual, Periodical (FDAP) payments to non-U.S. persons (ongoing) |
| Address offshore and cross-border compliance risks through enforcement and by issuing published guidance | • Completed project on foreign athletes and entertainers to ensure appropriate reporting and sourcing of income<br>• Completed voluntary settlement initiative for embassy/consular employees and continuing to pursue enforcement activities on non-electors<br>• Issued regulations on transfer pricing, foreign tax credits, cross-border restructuring, and other cross-border issues |

## Component 5: Enhance Taxpayer Service

Providing quality taxpayer service is critical to protecting the approximately $2.7 trillion that U.S. taxpayers report and remit. The tax code is complex, and effective taxpayer assistance is necessary to help taxpayers understand and comply with their obligations.

### *Providing Innovative Online Services*

The demand for online services continues to grow dramatically. In FY 2008, *IRS.gov* received 2.2 billion web page visits, an increase of 74 percent from FY 2005. From January 1 to May 31, 2009, 48 million taxpayers used the "Where's My Refund?" web site, up from 24 million for the same period in 2005.

In FY 2008, the IRS launched a hybrid online/in-person service with its Facilitated Self-Assistance Research Project. This project provides a kiosk with web access at IRS Taxpayer Assistance Centers. The kiosk computers allow taxpayers to help themselves and to get additional help from an IRS assistor if needed. Through FY 2009, the IRS has installed kiosk services in 50 Taxpayer Assistance Centers.

### *Streamline Written Communications with Taxpayers*

In 2008, the IRS created a Taxpayer Communications Task Group to study and improve the clarity, accuracy, and effectiveness of written communications to taxpayers. Simple, clear communication makes it easier for taxpayers to comply with their obligations. While the work of the group is ongoing, an early success was the elimination of nearly a dozen inserts in a notice informing businesses that they owe additional tax. This change to the CP 161 notice, which is mailed to business taxpayers who underpay their taxes, will halt the mailing of tens of millions of pieces of paper, reduce taxpayer and preparer burden, and save the government money.

### *Taxpayer Assistance Blueprint*

The IRS continues to make progress in executing the initiatives outlined in its strategic plan for taxpayer service, the Taxpayer Assistance Blueprint (TAB). The TAB, which will be updated in the summer of 2009, outlines a series of initiatives aimed at enhancing IRS service options across all delivery channels: in person, on the Internet, and over the phone. The IRS has also embedded the philosophy and priorities of the TAB concept of improving service from the taxpayer perspective in every service improvement decision.

### *Status Update*

The following chart provides an update on the status of the taxpayer service initiatives currently underway or completed since the release of prior tax gap reports:

| Action Items | Status |
|---|---|
| Increase accuracy on toll-free telephone customer inquiries, processing functions, and paper adjustments | • Implementing and deploying Interactive<br>• Tax Law Assistant tool to provide accurate, efficient, and complete<br>• responses to basic tax law inquiries (in process) |
| | • Implementing and deploying Accessory<br>• Manager tools that provide standard research paths, consolidate account data, and automatically populate input fields (in process)<br>• Implemented recommendations from the<br>• Correspondence Accuracy Improvement<br>• Study |
| Enhance IRS.gov | • Deployed interactive tax law decision support tool in FY 2009 filing season that includes enhanced FAQs<br>• Preparing interactive probe and response capabilities (in process) |
| Improve the quality of volunteer-prepared returns through enhancements to the VITA program, including quality training and sample processing reviews | • Conducted on-site workshops to address quality concerns, and revised the volunteer return preparation training to use a process based training (PBT) approach for all volunteers.<br>• Incorporating PBT concepts into online volunteer training application: Link & Learn Taxes (in process) |
| Enhance services to persons with limited English proficiency (LEP) through the Taxpayer Assistance Blueprint, development of a Multi-Lingual Strategic Plan, development of a Virtual Translation Office, and launch of a revised version of the Spanish IRS.gov webpage | • Added enhancements including "Where's My Refund?", "How Much Was My Economic Stimulus Payment?", and the Economic Stimulus Calculator to the Spanish IRS.gov |

| Action Items | Status |
|---|---|
| | • Undertook research efforts to pinpoint isolated community locations and identify actions to customize assistance<br>• Performed targeted outreach for LEP taxpayers<br>• Expanded Virtual Translation Office to provide tax forms, publications, and education materials in Spanish and other IRS-priority languages |
| Improve quality and timeliness of taxpayer contacts by maintaining an enhanced integrated quality assurance process with internal and external partners | • Developed and deployed Site Coordinator's Training, mandating use of intake and interview sheets and quality reviews for all return preparation.<br>• Continued partner and employee feedbackvia roundtable discussions and partner satisfaction surveys<br>• Implemented a Quality Statistical Sample Cadre to perform on-site return reviews that incorporates a second level review |
| Improve services through programs at both the national and local level by expanding collaborations with organizations serving the disabled, Native American communities, and pre-existing rural infrastructures | • Increased availability of free tax return preparation and financial/EITC education through a network of national and local partners in hard-to-serve Native Americancommunities as well as for low income disabled persons<br>• Working with Department of Agriculture and Rural Funding Foundations to increase availability of tax-related services in rural communities<br>• Established measures to gauge national and local penetration rates for the rural initiative and shared best practices with rural partners |
| Expand and enhance the Spanish Website to increase electronic options, including options for Spanish language delivery of applications currently only in English | • Added "Where's My Refund?", "How Much Was My Economic Stimulus Payment?", and the Economic Stimulus Calculator to the Spanish website |

**(Continued)**

| Action Items | Status |
|---|---|
| | • Expanded and enhanced taxpayer education information including tax responsibilities and eligibility requirements for various credits and other benefits |
| Provide Reporting Agents with access to e-Services | • Deployed access to Electronic Account Resolution (EAR) and Transcript DeliverySystem (TDS) for Reporting Agents |
| Implement Taxpayer Assistance Blueprint Phase 2, which includes a five-year strategic plan for taxpayer service based on extensive research to understand taxpayer and stakeholder needs | • Embedded the TAB Guiding Principles within the FY 2009-2013 IRS Strategic Plan<br>• Issuing in summer 2009 the second annualReport to Congress, which will include examples of numerous taxpayer service improvements accomplished in 2008 and 2009 |
| Implement Internet-Customer Account Services (I-CAS) Release 1, which will enable taxpayer to view account information | • Working toward electronic access to account information, once all data securityissues are resolved and the core taxpayer account database complete |
| Implement I-CAS Release 2, which will enable taxpayers to change their address, file an extension, submit a Power of Attorney, and calculate a payoff amount on balances due via a secure Internet link | • Status is same as above |
| Continue publicity efforts encouraging use of Online Payment Agreement (OPA) | • Issued new releases and other communications during filing seasons, including directions for accessing OPA from IRS.gov<br>• Worked with tax software providers and other stakeholders to promote OPA |
| Enable taxpayers with disabilities to understand available tax credits and receive tax preparation assistance through partnerships with national and local organizations that serve this unique group of taxpayers | • Partnering with national and local organizations, including government entities, to increase return preparation services |

## Component 6: Reform and Simplify the Tax Law

Earlier this year, the President's Economic Recovery Advisory Board (PERAB) formed a Task Force on Tax Reform. The task force will, among other things, focus on tax simplification. The task force will report back to the board, and the full board is expected to report back to the President with options.

The following is a more detailed listing of specific action items that are underway by the IRS and Treasury to reform and simplify the tax law.

| Initiatives | Work with Congress to enact simplification legislative provisions |
|---|---|
| Continue Taxpayer Burden Reduction projects | • Released revised Forms 1120S and 2553, along with related regulation changes, to simplify an S Corporation election<br>• Released revised Form 94X, along with related regulation changes, to reduce employment tax reporting errors<br>• Released new Form 8857 for innocent spouse relief |
| Continue tax form and publication improvements | • Among other improvements, developed a multi-year prioritized plan of burden reduction activities to include forms redesign and simplification, defined the MeF platform for XML-enabled PDF Form 1040, and launched a hyperlinked Publication 17, Your Federal Income Tax, on IRS.gov |

## Component 7: Coordinate with Partners and Stakeholders

### *Tax Return Preparer Review*

The IRS recently announced that, by the end of 2009, the Commissioner will propose a comprehensive set of recommendations concerning tax return preparers. The review seeks to identify ways to improve taxpayer compliance and to ensure strong and uniform ethical standards of conduct for tax preparers.

Potential recommendations could focus on a new model for the regulation of tax return preparers, improved service and outreach for return preparers, education and training for return preparers, and enforcement related to return preparer misconduct.

The tax return preparer review will begin with a fact-finding effort targeted at a large and diverse constituent community, including both licensed tax preparers—such as enrolled agents, lawyers and accountants—and unlicensed tax preparers and software vendors. The effort will also seek input and dialogue with consumer groups and taxpayers.

### *Enhanced Collaboration with Partners and Stakeholders*

The IRS has strengthened its partnerships with other state and Federal agencies. Strong collaboration enables the IRS and its partner agencies to make more efficient and effective use of existing resources. For example, the IRS has undertaken initiatives to make better use of information from state agencies, including state audit reports, and has developed a coordinated strategy to combat employment tax schemes.

Finally, the IRS has expanded its partnership with stakeholders to communicate more effectively with the numerous constituencies whose efforts might help raise the level of voluntary compliance.

Examples include work with the Small Business Administration to educate new business owners on key tax topics, and expanded work with partners to communicate with military retirees on retirement-related tax issues.

### *Status Update*

The following chart provides a status update on coordination efforts currently underway or completed since the release of prior tax gap studies:

| Action Items | Status |
|---|---|
| Enhance the centralized process to maximize utilization of State Audit Reports (SARs) by IRS for federal assessments | • Established a system to establish baseline usability and productivity of incoming SARs<br>• Continue to partner with states to implement enhancements (including automation of receipts) to improve usability of SARs |
| Implement a Questionable Employment Tax Practices (QETP) Initiative in partnership with the Department of Labor, National Association of State Workforce Agencies, Federation of Tax Administrators, and state workforce agencies to provide a collaborative national approach to combat employment tax schemes | • Implemented initiative with initial 20 states participating, with 25 percent participation increases targeted and achieved in FY08 and FY09<br>• Incorporated data provided by the states into employment tax audit work streams |

| Action Items | Status |
|---|---|
| Further enhance the Fed/Fed program by facilitating and expanding partnerships with other Federal agencies to improve tax administration | • Expanded partnerships to include the Social Security Administration (SSA) andthe Small Business Administration (SBA) |
| Engage all 50 states through the State Reverse File Match Initiative (SRFMI) – a process that matches IRS extracts received through the Governmental Liaison Data Exchange Program against state master files to identify individuals and businesses who filed a state return but not a federal return and to identify differences in federal and state income reporting | • Engaged in 2008 pilot use of systemic SRFMI data received from 14 states, and increased state agency participation to 44 agencies in 2009<br>• Expansion in process |
| Determine tax administration benefits of utilizing state data warehouse concept | • Evaluating internal systems such as Compliance Data Warehouse and Integrated Production Model to determine feasibility |
| Develop an educational targeted outreach DVD for military personnel preparing for retirement | • Distributed and integrated DVD into all military pre-retirement seminars to ensure retirees understand tax rules applicable to their retirement benefits<br>• Working with Department of Labor to include a topic on withholding taxes as a requirement for all military retiree trainingconducted on military bases and developing a Life Cycle Brochure on this topic for distribution |
| Enhance outreach efforts to industry audiences about available Audit Technique Guides and Tax Tips | • Determined what enhancements to current guides and what new guides are needed<br>• Continued to publicize availability of guides via national and local liaison activities |
| Establish links to IRS.gov on industry, practitioner, educational, and governmental stakeholder websites | • Established Tax Centers (dedicated web space) with links to state and national organization websites |
| Develop and widely distribute educational fact sheets on areas of high noncompliance | • Distributed monthly fact sheets on wide variety of subject matters including avoiding incorrect self-employment deductions, wage compensation for S Corporation officers, and managing paper and electronic recordkeeping requirements |

**(Continued)**

| Action Items | Status |
|---|---|
| Develop a strategy to reach practitioners without affiliation to a professional organization | • Developed grass-roots delivery channel with national retail tax preparation firms, expanded outreach to colleges and universities to include graduates entering tax field |
| Leverage key partners such as the SBA and its SCORE program and Small Business Development Centers (SBDCs) to deliver small business workshops to the new business community | • Continued contact with traditional partners to maximize leveraged opportunities that provide education and outreach directly to business owners<br>• Partnered with SCORE and SBDCs to enhance quality and consistency of leveraged Small Business Tax Workshops<br>• Partnered with SBA to increase outreach through the National Women's Business Council in order to promote voluntary compliance and share information customized for new business owners<br>• Increased the number of Small Business Tax Workshops |
| Deliver educational messages through existing relationships with universities and colleges | • Expanding participation of current Historically Black Colleges and Universities (HBCUs) in the VITA program (in process)<br>• Increasing participation of Beta Alpha Psi,national scholastic and professional fraternity, in VITA program by 10% (in process)<br>• Expanding the Cooperative Extension Services Network tax prep and education program in each of the four regions, HBCUs, tribal colleges and universities (in process) |
| Develop audio educational messages for toll-free wait times | • Developed text and appropriate placement of specific educational messages<br>• Deploying audio educational messages (expected July 2009) |

| Action Items | Status |
|---|---|
| Customize outreach to specific industries to encourage voluntary compliance | • Launched industry specific communication and outreach to small businesses, industry stakeholders, and state licensing agencies<br>• Performing outreach in all states to promote use of IRS's web-based Tax Centers designed to provide education andweb resources for specific industries and professions (in process)<br>• Provided educational materials to new andexisting business owners through partnerships with small business and industry stakeholders and state licensing agencies in all 50 states |
| Request feedback from internal and external stakeholders on existing outreach and educational programs to identify best practices and enhancements | • Convened IRS-wide task force to collect and review stakeholder feedback, shared recommendations with external stakeholders, and obtained additional feedback (implementation of recommendations ongoing) |
| Develop strategies to educate first-time business filers | • Implemented outreach strategy to first-time business filers including collaboration with small business and industry partners to develop an outreach campaign to educate first time Schedule C filers, including common errors to avoid |
| Expand relationships and collaboration with foreign tax administrations to increase informal and formal communications on international tax administration matters | • Completed OECD project relating to international guidelines on attribution of profits to permanent establishments<br>• Participating in OECD work on monitoring Transfer Pricing Guidelines, including international business restructurings (ongoing)<br>• Negotiated protocols to income tax treaties with Luxembourg and Switzerlandto make the exchange of information provisions consistent with U.S. and OECD standards<br>• |

**(Continued)**

| Action Items | Status |
|---|---|
| | • Continuing efforts to conclude tax information exchange agreements, including agreements recently signed with Liechtenstein and Gibraltar<br>• Participating in the Leeds Castle Group with the tax administration agencies of China, India, South Korea, the United Kingdom, Japan, Australia, Canada, France, and Germany (ongoing)<br>• Collaborating via the Joint International Tax Shelter Information Centre (JITSIC) with Canada, Australia, and the United Kingdom to identify and curb abusive tax avoidance transactions (ongoing)<br>• • Participating with the OECD working group on Aggressive Tax Planning to design a database of various cross-border tax avoidance schemes (ongoing) |

# V. IRS Strategic Plan

Since the publication of the last tax gap report, the IRS published a new *strategic plan* for FY 2009-2013. The strategic plan outlines the service and enforcement goals of the IRS, along with the strategic foundations that underpin both. The plan recognizes that the IRS must excel at both service and enforcement: success is not an either/or proposition. The plan also outlines five longterm measures for evaluating the IRS's progress in achieving its goals, and which directly relate to the tax gap strategy. Those measures, some of which have been discussed above, include the following:

- Voluntary Compliance Rate. The Voluntary Compliance Rate, as explained earlier in this report, is highlighted in the strategic plan as a key long-term measure. The IRS's goal is to achieve an 86 percent voluntary compliance rate for Tax Year 2009, and is actively pursuing updates to the tax gap estimates that will allow progress against this goal to be measured.

- E-File Rate. The IRS has been tracking the rate of electronic filing for individual income tax returns since the inception of electronic filing in 1986, reporting the number of individual tax returns (Form 1040) that have been filed electronically in its published performance reports. The IRS is currently seeking to achieve an 80 percent e-file rate by 2012 for all major tax returns filed with the IRS.
- ACSI All Individual Taxpayer Score. The American Customer Satisfaction Index (ACSI) is a national indicator of customer satisfaction with the quality of products and services available to consumers in the United States. Each December, the ACSI issues a report on satisfaction of recipients of services from the Federal government. In 1999, the Federal government selected the ACSI to be a standard metric for measuring citizen satisfaction. Agency participation is voluntary but relatively extensive. Over 55 Federal government agencies have used the ACSI to measure citizen satisfaction of more than 110 services and programs. The IRS performance measure focuses on the satisfaction score associated with all individual income tax filers (paper and electronic filers). The IRS has a goal of achieving a satisfaction score of 72 for the 2012 tax year. As discussed above, a taxpayer-friendly tax filing process is essential to improving compliance.
- Nonrevenue Enforcement Activity. IRS has developed an index of enforcement activities that promote compliance yet do not focus primarily on tax revenue. IRS examines changes in this index in order to assess trends in its nonrevenue performance, which is similar to using the Consumer Price Index to assess trends in consumer prices. The nonrevenue enforcement activity index includes examination activity in the Tax Exempt and Government Entities Division as well as Bank Secrecy Act investigations.
- Employee Engagement. A motivated, well-trained, and dedicated workforce is critical to the ultimate success of all IRS initiatives. The IRS for several years has been conducting an annual employee survey to obtain feedback on a wide range of workplace issues. The results are used to calculate an engagement index, which is compared with engagement scores from prior years and from other agencies.

Recognizing the importance of a well-trained workforce to the accomplishment of the goals and metrics outlined in the strategic plan, the IRS last summer launched a Workforce of Tomorrow Task Force. The Task Force's goal is to ensure that, five years from now, the IRS has a workforce equipped to serve America's taxpayers for the next fifteen years. The Task Force produced a roadmap of initiatives to address the IRS's greatest workforce challenges, which includes 58 recommendations that are currently being implemented. The IRS workforce is the foundation for the ultimate success of its efforts to implement its strategic plan and reduce the tax gap.

## CONCLUSION

The tax gap imposes an unfair burden on law-abiding taxpayers, and the Department of the Treasury and the IRS are committed to narrowing the gap between what is owed and what is paid. This report has highlighted new initiatives to improve tax revenue collection, both through improved voluntary compliance and through effective enforcement. It has also provided status updates on a full range of initiatives currently underway or completed since the release of previous tax gap reports.

As outlined above, the plan to reduce the tax gap has multiple parts. Targeted changes in the tax laws, enhanced taxpayer service, and increased enforcement are all critical to this effort. As this report describes, progress has already been made with respect to key strategic priorities and initiatives, both those identified in prior tax gap reports and those developed since the issuance of the last report. In order to provide accurate and up-to-date assessments of progress, Treasury and IRS are deploying significant resources toward the long-term effort to produce regular, updated estimates of the tax gap, which will be used to assess progress toward closing the tax gap.

The Administration's FY 2010 budget proposes an expansive set of additional tools and requirements to reduce opportunities for evasion and other non-compliance. The Administration is committed to working closely with Congress to strike an appropriate balance to maximize revenue collection without imposing unreasonable compliance and enforcement burdens on the vast majority of individuals and businesses that fully and willingly pay what they owe.

# APPENDIX: UNDERSTANDING THE TAX GAP[5]

The Internal Revenue Code places three primary obligations on taxpayers: (1) to file timely returns; (2) to make accurate reports on those returns; and (3) to pay the required tax voluntarily and timely. Taxpayers are compliant when they meet these obligations. Noncompliance — and the tax gap — results when taxpayers do not meet these obligations.

The tax gap is defined as the aggregate amount of true tax liability imposed by law for a given tax year that is not paid voluntarily and timely. True tax liability for any given taxpayer means the amount of tax that would be determined for the tax year in question if all relevant aspects of the tax law were correctly applied to all of the relevant facts of that taxpayer's situation. For a variety of reasons, this amount often differs from the amount of tax that a taxpayer reports on a return. The taxpayer might not understand the law, might make inadvertent mistakes, or might misreport intentionally.

To be paid voluntarily, a tax liability must be paid without direct IRS intervention. Taxpayers have the responsibility to determine and report their correct tax liability, and to make sure that amount is paid (whether through withholding, estimated tax payments, payments with a filed return, etc.). The IRS focuses its enforcement where it is needed most, but the overall rate of tax compliance in the United States is as high as it is because the vast majority of taxpayers meet their obligations with little or no involvement from the IRS. To be paid timely, a tax liability must be paid in full on or before the date on which all payments for the given tax year were legally due.

It is important to emphasize that IRS estimates of the tax gap are associated with the legal sector of the economy only. Although tax is due on income from whatever source derived, legal or illegal, the tax attributable to income earned from illegal activities is extremely difficult to estimate. Moreover, the government's interest in pursuing this type of noncompliance is, ultimately, to stop the illegal activity, not merely to tax it.

Although they are related, the tax gap is not synonymous with the "underground economy." Definitions of the "underground economy" vary widely. However, most people characterize it in terms of the value of goods and services that elude official measurement. Furthermore, there are some items in the "underground economy" that are not included in the tax gap (such as tax due on illegal-source income), and there are contributors to the tax gap that no one would include in the "underground economy" (such as the tax associated with overstated exemptions, adjustments, deductions, or credits, or with claiming the wrong filing status). The greatest area of overlap between these two concepts is sometimes called the "cash economy," in which income (usually of a business nature) is received in cash, which helps to hide it from taxation.

Equally important, the tax gap does not arise solely from tax evasion or cheating. It includes a significant amount of noncompliance due to tax law complexity that results in errors of ignorance, confusion, and carelessness. This distinction is important even though, at this point, the IRS does not have sufficient data to distinguish clearly the amount of noncompliance that arises from willful, as opposed to unintentional, mistakes. Moreover, the line between intentional and unintentional mistakes is often a grey one, particularly in areas such as basis reporting, where a taxpayer may know that his or her reporting is inaccurate but does not have ready access to accurate information. This is an area where additional research is needed to improve understanding.

## Measuring the Tax Gap

Historically, estimates of federal tax compliance were based on special studies, including the Taxpayer Compliance Measurement Program (TCMP), which covered income and self-employment taxes and groups of taxpayers, and consisted of line-by-line audits of random samples of returns. These studies provided the IRS with information on compliance trends and allowed the IRS to update audit selection formulas regularly. However, this method of data gathering was extremely burdensome on the taxpayers whose returns were selected. As a result of concerns raised by taxpayers, Congress, and other stakeholders, the last TCMP audits were done in 1988.

The IRS conducted several much narrower compliance studies between 1988 and 2001, but nothing that would provide a comprehensive perspective on the overall tax gap. Until recently, all of these subsequent estimates of the tax gap have been rough projections that basically assume no change in compliance rates among the major tax gap components even though the magnitude of these projections reflects growth in tax receipts in these major tax gap categories.

The NRP, which the IRS has used to estimate the most recent tax gap updates, arose out of a desire to find a less intrusive means of measuring tax compliance. The IRS used a focused statistical selection process that resulted in the selection of approximately 46,000 individual income tax returns for Tax Year (TY) 2001 — somewhat fewer than previous compliance studies, even though the population of individual tax returns had grown over time.

Like the compliance studies of the past, the NRP was designed to allow the IRS to meet certain objectives — to estimate the overall extent of reporting compliance among individual income tax filers and to update the audit-selection formulas. It also introduced several innovations designed to reduce the burden imposed on taxpayers whose returns were selected for the study.

The first NRP innovation was to compile a comprehensive set of data to supplement what was reported on the selected returns. The sources of the "case building" data included third-party information returns from payers of income (e.g., Form W-2 and Form 1099) and prior-year returns filed by taxpayers. Also, for the first time, the IRS added data on dependents obtained from various government sources, as well as data obtained from public records (e.g., current and prior addresses, real estate holdings, business registrations, and involvement with corporations). Together, these data reduced the amount of information requested from taxpayers, with some of the selected taxpayers not requiring any contact from the IRS. In effect, these data allowed the IRS to focus its efforts on return information that could not otherwise be verified. This pioneering approach was so successful it is being expanded in regular operational audit programs.

A second major NRP innovation was to introduce a "classification" process, whereby the randomly selected returns and associated case-building data were first reviewed by experienced auditors (referred to as classifiers) who identified not only which issues needed to be examined, but also the best way to handle each return in the sample. In this way, each return was either: (1) accepted as filed, without contacting the taxpayer at all (although, sometimes, minor adjustments were noted for research purposes); (2) selected for correspondence audit of up to three focused issues; or (3) selected for an in-person audit where there were numerous items that needed to be verified. In addition, the classifiers identified compliance issues that the auditor was required to evaluate, although the examiners had the ability to expand the audit to investigate other issues as warranted.

Other NRP innovations included streamlining the collection of data, providing auditors with new tools to detect noncompliance, and involving stakeholders (including representatives of tax professional associations) in the design and implementation of the study. Clearly, the NRP approach was much less burdensome on taxpayers than the old TCMP audits, which examined every line item on every return.

## Tax Gap Estimates

As noted above, for the 2001 tax year, the overall gross tax gap was estimated to be approximately $345 billion, corresponding to a noncompliance rate of 16.3 percent. After accounting for enforcement efforts and late payments, the amount was reduced to $290 billion, corresponding to a net noncompliance rate of 13.7 percent.

Noncompliance takes three forms:

- Not filing required returns on time (nonfiling);
- Not reporting one's full tax liability on a timely filed return (underreporting); and,
- Not timely paying the full amount of tax reported on a timely return (underpayment).

The IRS has separate tax gap estimates for each of these three types of noncompliance. Underreporting (in the form of unreported receipts and overstated expenses) constitutes over 82 percent of the gross tax gap, up slightly from earlier estimates. Underpayment constitutes nearly 10 percent and nonfiling almost 8 percent of the gross tax gap.

### *Nonfiling*

The nonfiling gap is defined as the amount of true tax liability that is not paid on time by taxpayers who do not file a required return on time (or at all). It is reduced by amounts paid on time, such as through withholding, estimated payments, and other credits. The nonfiler population does not include legitimate nonfilers (i.e., those who have no obligation to file).

### *Underreporting*

The underreporting gap is defined as the amount of tax liability not voluntarily reported by taxpayers who file required returns on time. For income taxes, the underreporting gap arises from three errors: underreporting taxable income, overstating offsets to income or to tax, and net math errors. Taxable income includes such items as wages and salaries, rents and royalties, and net business income. Offsets to income include income exclusions, exemptions, statutory adjustments, and deductions. Offsets to tax are tax *credits. Net* math errors involve arithmetic mistakes or transcription errors made by taxpayers that are corrected at the time the return is processed. In addition to developing an estimate of the aggregate underreporting gap, it is possible to break aspects of this estimate down into measures of the underreporting gap attributable to specific line items on the tax return.

### *Underpayment*

The underpayment gap is the portion of the total tax liability that taxpayers report on their timely filed returns but do not pay on time. This arises primarily from insufficient remittances from taxpayers themselves. However, it also includes employer under-deposits of withheld income tax. In the case of withheld income tax, it is the responsibility of the employees to report the corresponding tax liability on timely filed returns, and it is the responsibility of their employers to deposit those withholdings with the government on time.

## End Notes

1 "Comprehensive Strategy for Reducing the Tax Gap," U.S. Department of the Treasury, Office of Tax Policy, September 26, 2006.

2 "Reducing the Federal Tax Gap: A Report on Improving Voluntary Compliance," Internal Revenue Service, Department of the Treasury, August 2, 2007.

3 The IRS's top-level measures, goals, and timelines are published in the Appendix to its strategic plan, available at http://www.irs.gov/pub//newsroom/long_term_measures.pdf

4 "Advancing E-file Study Phase 1 Report: Achieving the 80% E-file Goal Requires Partnering with Stakeholders on New Approaches to Motivate Paper Filers," Internal Revenue Service, Department of the Treasury, September 30, 2008.

5 This section is reproduced from "Reducing the Federal Tax Gap: A Report on Improving Voluntary Compliance," Internal Revenue Service, Department of the Treasury, August 2, 2007, pp. 6-9.

# INDEX

## M



## N



## O



## P



## Q

## X



## Y